Heavenly Tidings
&
Railway Sidings

*Viewing the world from a favourite perspective
(The Ffestiniog Railway between Blaenau Ffestiniog
and Porthmadog)*

Heavenly Tidings
&
Railway Sidings

STUART SAMUEL

A Memoir

Crumps Barn Studio

For J

Crumps Barn Studio LLP
Crumps Barn, Syde, Cheltenham GL53 9PN
www.crumpsbarnstudio.co.uk

Cover design by Lorna Gray © Crumps Barn Studio
Cover photograph © Stuart Samuel
Photographic plates © Stuart Samuel

ISBN 978-1-9998705-8-4

About the Author

Stuart Samuel is a retired parish priest. Formerly, he has served in parishes throughout Yorkshire, Leicestershire and Linconshire.

Trains, both diesel and steam, have always been his passion and they have led him on many unforgettable journeys.

Stuart lives in North Wales with his wife. This is his first book.

I'm told that my first word was neither 'Papa' nor 'Mama' but 'Tan' – which, being translated means, 'Please, I'd like to examine that photographic equipment around your neck.' Spoken at a rather quiet Belle Vue in Manchester in 1950

Chapter 1

The Beginning

I'm informed I first saw light of day at 2am on Tuesday 7th September 1948 in Halifax General Hospital in Yorkshire – and unwittingly made the American Labor Day (which fell the day before) assume personal significance for my mother, Ella Samuel.

My parents were living in Boothtown, Halifax at the time, since their marriage at the parish church in 1945.

My father's full name was John Hedley Rees Samuel. He hailed originally from Gorseinon in South Wales. The taxman called him John, his parents called him Hedley, no one called him Rees, and because having three forenames was clearly insufficient, everyone else drew to mind his ancestry and called him 'Taffy' or 'Taff' (although he swore to his dying day that he knew nothing about that missing beef).

He was working for Percy Shaw, the eccentric inventor of the reflecting road-stud or 'cats' eyes', which made a big contribution towards road safety and an even bigger contribution towards Percy Shaw's bank balance, especially during the dark nights of the blackouts of World War II.

Both my parents were from working class backgrounds – when they met during the war, my mother was a seamstress and my father was serving in the RAF. One weekend, finding himself with leave and nothing particular to do, he was invited by his RAF friend Lawrence Jackson to accompany him to Halifax to meet his sister, Ella. And the rest, as they say, is history, with a Welsh-Yorkshire alliance being cemented in 1945.

Chapter 2

Early Years

Halifax had suffered little from the hands of the Luftwaffe compared with the neighbouring cities of Bradford and Leeds, but they were lean days for most people in the aftermath of World War II.

We lived first in a pokey little rented property in Sutcliffe Buildings, Sowerby Bridge. These were back-to-back houses, with one row of housing facing the main road and the other, where we lived, having a view over the Calder Valley. But this was hardly a view to die for, as, when you looked over the valley towards the town of Sowerby Bridge, you saw only a huge dirty plume of smoke from the many mill chimneys of the industrial town.

Added to that was the stench of the tip in the river valley, the noise from the sawmill and the noise and smoke from countless freight trains, chuffing away from the coalfields of South Yorkshire, delivering coal to the

Lancashire towns.

So I was rocked to sleep by the wagons laden with coal, being dragged along 60ft lengths of railway line by clanking War Department 2-8-0 steam locomotives. I grew up to love railways, and it's interesting to note that although there was an almost continual procession of these trains in those days (with their corresponding lines of empty wagons rattling by in the opposite direction), only one WD 2-8-0 has survived into preservation, on the Keighley & Worth Valley Railway.

Sutcliffe Buildings were poor houses in which to bring up a child, for the lie of the land meant there were also some one-storey houses under ours at the back, so we had neither garden nor backyard – just a narrow, railed landing around the block, leading from our only outer door, to the main road at the front, the dustbins in a small alcove, along with the lavatories. If you were caught short in the middle of the night, the chamber pot was your friend.

At first, there was no electricity in the house – only gas. Our evenings were filled with my father trying to read the local newspaper, the Halifax Courier. My mother would be knitting and I would be listening to the battery-powered wireless. The room was almost lit by the yellowish tinge of the one gas mantel, until it popped, plunging us into darkness. Then it was, 'where're the candles?' and, 'you did buy some new mantles, didn't you?'

Today, we would call it atmospheric mood lighting but then it was absolutely horrible.

There was an open fire, upon which we burned normal coal (certainly not smokeless then). It had to be brought in by the bucket from the coal store at the end of the landing near the lavatories. If you could arrange it so that the fire was running down just about the same time as you needed to visit the loo, then you could combine the two objects of the journey and at least gain the satisfaction of achieving a certain economy of movement. Oh, the simple pleasures of those days.

The fire was also needed to heat the water, so plenty of coal was needed on a Friday night, when the tin bath was taken down from its hook in the kitchen, and after being filled in front of the fire, the Order of the Bath would begin. Father first, because he was the bread-winner, and I suppose regarded as the muckiest, then Mother, then last but not least, me. By that time I was extremely fortunate if the water was wet, let alone plentiful, hot or clean. But, poor as we were, I always had a bath on a Friday night, whether I needed it or not.

One of my favourite toys when I was four or five, was

a tin pedal car in which I sat and pedalled to my heart's content up and down the landing – the passage that ran past our front door. This car was about 2ft wide, and the landing about 2ft 6 inches. Consequently it took at lot of skill to navigate it from one end to the other. Any slight misjudgement, and you clanged into the railings or the houses, and the plaintive cry of 'mind my b— drainpipe' was the neighbours' default acknowledgement of my lack of driving skills.

I was a bit of a boy-racer (I got it out of my system at an early age), and also showed remarkable determination even then, for once I embarked upon my journey, I yielded for no one – whether human or feline. Anyone trying to exit their house had to draw back in again very quickly when they saw me coming, and any cat over 3 inches wide quickly realised their only escape was to wriggle through the railings down the 10 ft drop to the ground below. It was then I noticed that cats nearly always manage to land on their feet, and, apart from their pride being hurt, they were unscathed by their experience.

The neighbours must in fact have been extremely forgiving of my rallying, for I survived to tell the tale. I was, after all, the only child on the landing, and I suppose, as such, a bit of a novelty value. The cats, though, were not so accommodating. They patiently bided their time until thirty or so years later when I was married to a wife who insisted on rescuing any stray in the neighbourhood which cared to walk up our drive. We ended up with a very full house. Feline karma is like that.

So these were some of the memories of my early childhood. A poor back-to-back house (now demolished as they were regarded as a fire risk), no indoor sanitation, an open coal fire, no electricity (until the landlord grudgingly supplied this new-fangled stuff when we'd lived there a few years or so). Lethal town gas, lead water pipes, and a drop of some 10ft through the railings. By today's standards, I was lucky to survive.

The famous tin pedal car – not very much wider than the landing itself. Woe betide anyone foolish enough to wish to walk in the other direction at the same time. Note the look of determination on the face, and the couple of felines in the background, wisely considering escape through the railings

Chapter 3

On the Up

I remember the year 1953 very clearly, for one day the neighbours got together and decorated our humble little landing with flags and bunting. This was in honour, as I realised later, of the Coronation of Queen Elizabeth II. Also, more importantly at the time to me, I'm afraid, the year is fixed in my memory as the moment that sweets came off the ration.

During WWII and afterwards various items of foodstuffs and clothing were rationed. You registered with a draper, grocer, butcher, sweet shop, etc of your choice, and they were supplied with the correct amount of rationed goods for each person on their lists. You received a Ration Book, holding a certain number of stamps for each particular item, and those stamps were removed or cancelled when a purchase was made. Once your stamps had been invalidated, that was it for the period under review. And the monthly sweet ration was between 8 and

16 ozs, depending on the severity of the shortage at the time.

8 ounces! How was a growing boy supposed to survive on one chocolate bar per month, even though my parents generously allowed me their ration too? But come February 5th, I could be taken into any sweetshop and exchange my pocket money for as many dolly-mixtures and toffees as the money would buy.

I believe this date also marked a time when dentists throughout the land rubbed their hands as queues for NHS dentistry developed overnight . . .

As my father was the only bread-winner, holidays were day-trips to Blackpool or Belle Vue Manchester by 'chara' or train – whichever was the cheaper. 'Chara' was the colloquial name for the bus – it was only later I realised it was short for 'charabanc', a word I probably couldn't have spelt then, even if I had been familiar with it.

A journey on it to Blackpool was a three hour marathon via the winding local roads, with a stop for toilets at Whalley. The return journey was even longer, as the toilet stop became an extended pub break, when there were always a few passengers determined to spend whatever they had remaining from the funfair and slot machines of Blackpool promenade on the variety of liquid refreshment the landlord had to offer.

The driver would be desperately trying to pull them out after half an hour or so, while the children remained on the bus, placated by the occasional packet of Smith's crisps.

The train was better, though more expensive. We arrived at Blackpool's Central station, a massive complex right next door to the Tower. The first task on arrival was to join the queue for the toilets after a two hour journey on a non-corridor train (normally), and then there was the short distance to Woolworth's cafeteria for fish and chips, followed by the even shorter walk dodging trams and donkeys onto the sands.

When I was five, I was enrolled at Bolton Brow Infants School, just up the road from where we lived. My one abiding memory of this establishment was an enforced sleep every afternoon. There were lessons in the morning, then dinner (this was the North of England, remember!). Then, after playtime, camp beds were assembled in the classroom and we had to lie down and sleep between 1.30pm and 2.30pm. Lastly it would be story-time – being read to by the teacher until going home time at 3.15pm.

I suppose the enforced nap was in keeping with the latest educational theories of the time, but I found it difficult. I wanted to be up and about, doing things.

However, it was to stand me in good stead, for the wisdom of years has brought a growing realisation of the need for a siesta after lunch, and the day is incomplete without it. Indeed, and I'm jumping ahead many years now, one of my tutors at theological college used to say, 'When I wake up, if I'm in my pyjamas it's time for Mass. If not, it's time for tea.'

In 1956, upon the death of my paternal grandfather, who I never really knew, my father inherited the sum of £200, which he promptly put as the deposit on a house in the cleaner and fresher Spring Wood Avenue, Copley Lane. The house was a palace of recent build, and had a garden, electricity throughout and an inside bathroom and toilet!

It cost £1760, and with the help of the Halifax Building Society we moved there in 1957, where we celebrated our moving-in by hiring a black and white TV set with 2 channels, BBC and ITV, from DER – 'Domestic Electrical Rentals' to give it its official trading name – and I was enrolled at Copley Primary School.

My mother then took up work as an usherette at the Cinema Royal in Halifax. I can remember at least six traditional cinemas in a town the size of Halifax. In those days before the popularity of TV and home entertainment, picture houses abounded. She enjoyed that job immensely – walking up and down with her torch, shushing people and putting strange men in their place.

She did this in the afternoons, from curtain-up to 6pm. My school day finished at 3.45pm, but I was no latch-key kid. Rather, I was supplied daily with two pence for the 4pm Halifax Corporation No. 27 bus into town, where I waited outside the side door 'exit only' (no handle on the outside – 'Push bar to open' on the inside), to be admitted by my mother at 4.15pm, thereby neatly bypassing the pay kiosk.

Anyone just passing by might have been concerned to see a young boy standing in the alcove only for the door to suddenly open outwards, and a hand reach out and yank the boy in, followed by the door closing and his not being seen again. But those were more innocent times, and, as far as I know, the police were never called.

In the meanwhile, I was settling down to watch the last hour of the film. Consequently, I was well acquainted with the endings of blockbusters such as *The Cruel Sea, The Dam Busters* or *The Ladykillers,* but I still don't know to this day how they started.

My mother had cinema in her blood. Her father, Ernest Jackson, had been a cinema projectionist, and had worked in most of the town's establishments. There was more to this job than simply starting the film and then twiddling your thumbs for a couple of hours. A long film needed two or more spools and two projectors, and the art was in having the first working and pointing through the hole to the screen, and the second primed with the next spool and ready to run, so that when the first spool ended, the projector was swiftly moved to one side and replaced by the second, without the join being detected.

I think there was a slight overlap in the films, but it was still an exacting task, requiring the projectionist, as well as the projector, to remain focussed. Get it right, and no one noticed – your skill being taken for granted. Misjudge it, and you were rewarded by stamping and jeering from the gentlemen of the audience.

A popular film in my grandfather's time was the 1927 Alfred Hitchcock thriller *The Lodger – A Story of the London Fog*. This was remade in 1953 under the title *The Man in the Attic,* but people still referred to it by its original name. I remember once a woman stopped my mother in town and asked, 'Have you got *The Lodger* at your place?'

'No,' Mother replied, 'but spend half an hour in the front stalls and you're bound to get one …'

*Surveying the view from my pushchair outside the Post
Office on Commercial St in Halifax, being propelled
by my mother, Ella, and her mother Anne in reserve.
Notice that even at that stage I was not content to ride
facing the engine, but liked to see where I was going*

*Proud to take delivery of my first car when 22 months
old on a family trip to Blackpool. I was not pleased to to
find the showman wanted it back afterwards*

Chapter 4

Yorkshire Wool

My father, in the meanwhile, was working in the wool processing industry at Bridge End Dyeworks in Elland. Sheep were plentiful on those rugged slopes of the Pennines, in fact it was one of the main forms of farming. He was involved in the early stages, when the fleeces were delivered to the dyeworks in large canvas bags. They were dirty and greasy, and the first job was to scour (wash) them in large vats of water heated to 60°C, to which detergent was added. The wool was then rinsed several times and the dirty water was released directly into the River Calder located conveniently outside the window – not recommended for outdoor swimming, but the accepted practice of the day.

The vats were up to 20ft wide and 10ft deep, and loaded/unloaded manually, which was hard work as the wet wool was very heavy. The wool was then transferred to other similar vats, again by strength of human arms, for dyeing. This was achieved by juggling a mixture of dyes and chemicals (probably most of them banned by now), and the whole lot being heated again and left until the right shade was achieved.

It was always an anxious moment when a sample was taken into the office and examined carefully under a special daylight bulb against the colour card supplied by the customer. If it matched, the kettle went on and a celebratory mug of tea was enjoyed. If not, it was back to the bottles of dyes and chemicals and the formula revisited, accompanied by much unpaid overtime.

When it finally matched, it was approved by the Quality Control Manager – in effect the worker who was the least colour-blind of the bunch. It would then be lifted out of the vat and pushed in huge wagons to the drying room. Gym membership was not a necessary expense in the workers' budget.

Pride of place in the drying room was given to a huge spin-dryer. This was about 30 times the size of your domestic spinner at home, but using the same principle. It was commonly called 'The Woozer' and after watching its gyrations for the next ten minutes or so, it was not only the wool that was woozy. After this time, the power was cut off and a large brake handle applied. You leant against that for a few minutes or so, until the thing slowly juddered to a halt. Then the wool was loaded, again by hand, from the woozer to the dryer – a large conveyor-belt passing through heating elements in a scaled-up version of the toasters that are sometimes seen in self-service breakfast bars of hotels.

This used an enormous amount of electricity, and had the propensity to catch fire with the heat, dust and stray woollen fibres around. The wool was then loaded into yet another cart and pushed to the baling area, where it was baled and covered, ready for transportation, probably by the same lorry which had delivered the raw wool a few days previously. A regular customer was Crossley's – probably the best carpet manufacturer in the world – with a large factory in Halifax near North Bridge station (now an arts centre), to be woven into their best and shipped worldwide.

I think it gave my father a certain satisfaction to reflect that his handiwork was now being walked upon by important people around the globe.

Father spent most of his working life there, toiling for a mere pittance in extremes of heat and cold, facing dangers from chemicals, machinery and river (he fell in once, trying to clear a waste pipe). In fact I remember his joy on coming home on a Friday after about ten years of working there, with the good news he was now 'on staff' with holiday pay and sick pay, and an assured salary of £20 per week.

My parents had arrived.

Chapter 5

Family Outings

With finance being a little easier, we decided to have our first full week's holiday away from home. This was something my father had longed for, but my mother was more hesitant. She preferred to return to the luxury of her own bed at night. However, she was eventually persuaded to give it a go, and we decided that as it was the first time we were really going to enjoy it by going to a foreign land, so we decided on Wales.

Adverts in the Sunday papers were scrutinised and we settled on sunny Rhyl. The brochure was sent for and received by post, and we chose what looked like a reasonable boarding house. Letters were written and a deposit sent by postal order.

Each Northern town had its own annual holiday week, when the machinery would be closed down, giving the maintenance engineers time to do any necessary work and the workers a well-deserved break. Halifax's holiday week always began on the second Saturday in July, and it was called 'Wakes Week'.

I think the name 'Wake' derived from celebrating the local saint's holy day, and as Halifax Parish Church (now Minster) was dedicated to St John the Baptist, whose Nativity is celebrated on June 24th. The Wake Holy Day became Wakes holidays, which, for convenience sake, were transferred to early July.

This meant that the whole town virtually closing down and, with Blackpool being the nearest resort, you felt particularly at home there as you were continually meeting your neighbours! So this year we were more adventurous, and went further afield.

We enjoyed it at the beginning, and I just remember we spent most of the time walking up and down the seafront from the amusement arcades near Woolworth's to the Pleasure Beach and Miniature Railway. Little did I know that some sixty years later I would be enjoying a happy retirement within 300 yards of that railway.

After the first few days, though, my mother became homesick and eventually nagged my father sufficiently for him to agree that we should return home early. No doubt this was done to the landlady's delight as she now had spare rooms she could re-let without refunding us, and my father's annoyance at good money wasted.

The journey out had been a joyful occasion of discovery, but the return was slightly different. My father was carrying two heavy cases down the long Platform 11 between Manchester Exchange and Victoria stations and getting grumpier by the minute, while my mother and I led the way, with Mother encouraging him with words such as, 'Do hurry up, Taff, or we'll miss our connection.'

That was our first, and last, family holiday away from home for longer than one day.

As an aside: I remember a long time later after Mother had died, after a decent period of mourning, my father announced that he was going to do something he'd been wanting to do for some time. He booked a coach tour of 7 night's duration to Bournemouth. But it was not the delight he was envisaging – after a day he was missing her desperately.

By the time my family took a day holiday at Cleethorpes in 1952 I'd already decided I wished to follow my father into the RAF. A good 3d's worth ride in anyone's money

Chapter 6

Growing up

I was progressing up the educational ladder. What was in those days the West Riding of Yorkshire still had the 11+, and I took it at Copley Primary School, narrowly missing a place at the town's Grammar School – Heath Grammar. Instead, I secured a place at the newly opened Halifax Technical High School, first crossing their threshold in September of 1960.

This school was intended to bridge the gap between the Grammar School and local Secondary schools, and was supposed to include academic learning along with the teaching of various manufacturing skills. It was richly endowed with metalwork laboratories, woodwork rooms and engineering-drawing labs, and I don't know why I was chosen, because I hadn't then – and have never gained – a manufacturing skill in my whole body.

Anything from IKEA which boasts a 'seven-year-old child' can assemble usually leads me to search for such a child, or leave it to my present wife, who, having an MA in Translation Studies, understands these things.

In the first term, we had compulsory woodwork every Friday morning, followed by metalwork in the second term. In woodwork we were supposed to learn how to make basic mortise and tenon joints – I was a disaster. I well remember my woodwork teacher examining my pathetic attempt before hurling it across the room with the words, 'Wood doesn't grow on trees, lad.'

It was obviously a well-practised party piece, and I resisted responding with the obvious.

We then progressed (if that is the right word in my case) to making a teapot stand, using our newly learned skills of joining two bits of wood together in a cross, and covering it with carefully cut formica.

Well, due to my absence of skills in joint-making and added inability to use a plane, the whole thing rocked alarmingly when anything heavy was placed upon it. All the same, I proudly took it home, and my mother, as mothers do, cooed loudly upon receipt of it as though it were the one thing she had been coveting to make her life complete.

She gave it pride of place on the tea table. And every time a hot teapot was placed upon it, it rocked and tea was spilt on to the clean white cloth and varnished table underneath.

However, she cherished that gift, as mothers do, and it was brought out on every occasion – until the day I left for university seven years later, when I suspect the first thing she did after seeing me off on the train was to hurl it into the bin, for I never saw it again, and modest wisdom prevented me from asking what had happened to it.

The Education Authorities soon realised they had got the balance of practical skills and academic studies badly wrong, and we found ourselves learning German, French, English Literature and other such subjects perched on stools, surrounded by drills, lathes and planes. Indeed, studying Shakespeare's *Richard II* in the metalwork laboratory gave new meaning to the verse in Act 1 Scene II, where the Duchess of Gloucester speaking to John of Gaunt refers to *'that mettle, that self-mould that fashion'd thee'*. The school gradually achieved Grammar School status, and is now North Halifax Grammar.

One of the subjects I particularly enjoyed was music. I had been exposed to classical music at an early age by my maternal grandfather, of the cinema projectionist fame.

Unfortunately, his marriage with my grandmother had ended in divorce, and so visits to him were difficult as he had remarried, and my grandmother was very bitter. But if nothing else, Mother was a great peacemaker, and so most Monday nights she took me to see him, and to at least get to know him.

We didn't say very much as most of the time was spent listening to the latest 33rpm gramophone record he'd purchased of Schubert or Beethoven being played on his state-of-the-art radiogram – usually with the volume turned as high as possible. What a good job the neighbours were deaf (even though they may not have been originally!).

This experience led me to theorise later in life, that music, like religion, is not drilled into a person, but drawn out of them, and my grandfather Ernest Jackson unwittingly let me bathe in good music, for it to be drawn out of me by a later teacher at the Technical High School, one Geoffrey Holden.

I don't know if Geoffrey is still alive, but I owe him a huge debt of gratitude, for taking on the unenviable task of trying to teach 3rd and 4th Years classical music, and for doing it by sitting us all down and playing Prokofiev's Classical Symphony. That was it. I later chose music as one of my 'O' level subjects – this in a school which had begun by giving priority to drilling holes in wood and drawing up building plans!

My one regret was not being able to take it on to

'A' level, as unfortunately the school had then not the resources to teach me. Geoffrey Holden encouraged me to develop my singing skills in the school choir, which I enjoyed immensely. When, one day, instead of a musical noise all I could offer was a croak, he was very comforting, simply advising me to leave the choir for six months or so, and then return as a bass. Which I did.

I now realise his singing tuition stood me in good stead for my later life when intoning the chants and responses (the *versicles)* that were part of my daily work – something I think I managed to do without putting the Fear of God into too many of the congregation.

Chapter 7

Out of School

My main interest was railways. We could hear the railway from my first childhood home in Sutcliffe Buildings, even if we couldn't see it for the smoke and fug. But our new house at Spring Wood Avenue, Copley Lane was not only adjacent the Sowerby Bridge to Bradford branch of the original Leeds and Yorkshire railway (L&Y) from Manchester Victoria to Leeds, but it could be seen as well as heard.

My interest in the late 50s and early 60s was especially excited by the introduction of the diesel multiple unit. This was a cleaner and swifter mode of transport compared with the steam-hauled trains which had chuffed along before, and, more importantly, one in which you could sit behind the glass screen separating you from the driver.

I loved to watch them operate the train and observe the track ahead. I think I eventually knew the site of every signal between Halifax and Manchester Victoria!

Certainly the drivers began to know me, and in those more relaxed times they would encourage any lad who showed an interest, and would often leave the sliding door between their cab and the train open, and when it was dark, or a Saturday afternoon when there were no suits around, I was invited into the cab to view the whole journey from the front end. I got to the stage where I knew the rosters of the friendly drivers, and chose their trains deliberately!

As soon as I was old enough to travel alone, my pocket money carried me on a lot of trains. I remember making several journeys by steam in those days. Halifax station was a joint station used by what was the L&Y (later London Midland Scottish, LMS) and the Great Northern railway (GNR).

One L&Y branch carried trains from Sowerby Bridge to Bradford/Leeds. The branch on the other side of the triangle travelled from Bradford to Huddersfield and Penistone.

Journeying north from Halifax, you could go to Bradford or Leeds. There were two lines to Bradford – the L&Y and GNR – and both went to Bradford Exchange station. I never did manage to ride the GNR branch, as this closed to passenger traffic in 1952, but I did watch the dismantling of the line at Holmfield eight years later from the playground of the Halifax Technical High School.

This line, leaving Halifax station to the left via North Bridge, was a steeply graded route via Ovenden, Holmfield and Queensbury to Bradford – so steeply graded that local train crews knew it as 'over the Alps'.

I remember reading a lovely story of a football excursion laid on from Halifax to Bradford via this GNR route. In those days before privatisation, there was plenty of rolling-stock marshalled at sidings up and down the land, some of which was used only once a week on an excursion to the seaside. It is different these days, of course. Trains are now extremely expensive and must earn their keep so the Train Operating Companies (TOCs) cannot afford to have unused spare coaches in sidings. Back then, on the Nationalised Railway, the coaches, often ancient non-corridor stock, were available for the coupling.

On this particular day, the story went that demand had far exceeded what had been provided, so more and more coaches were simply added to the train to accommodate all comers. Eventually it departed, seriously overloaded, with the engine at the front far from capable for the task.

They started the long climb from Halifax up to Queensbury, making very slow progress indeed, in fact hardly moving at some stages. Unfortunately, some of the passengers were well-lubricated from their sojourns in the local Halifax pubs before boarding the train, and, of course, the one thing missing on non-corridor coaches, was access to a lavatory.

By the time the train reached Ovenden, about 2 miles out, the call was becoming urgent, and the train was not booked to stop there. But the crawling speed of the train was such that several managed to jump off it whilst it passed slowly through, visit the urinal on the platform, and re-board the same train in a coach further down!

By the time they got to Bradford, the match had already started. This was the line I was born too late to experience.

My journeys by steam to Bradford were via the LMS line, which itself had been difficult to construct. From Halifax it passed through five tunnels – Beacon Hill, Hipperholme, Lightcliffe, Wyke and Bowling – within eight or so miles. From Bowling, the line dropped steeply down into Bradford Exchange, as Bradford was in the bottom of a basin.

Bradford Exchange was at the end of the line, so trains terminated there at that stage. There was a link to the Leeds line for trains starting from Bradford. The lines formed a triangle, with the third side being a cut-off passing from Bowling to Laisterdyke.

The cut-off enabled trains from Manchester and Halifax to run directly on to Leeds. So services to Leeds stopped at Low Moor and divided, with the front three coaches being taken down into Bradford by the engine which had brought the train from Manchester, and the rear three coaches being left behind, waiting for a tank engine to back down from the sheds, couple-up and proceed to Leeds. It took about ten minutes, but seemed an age when you were just waiting in Low Moor station.

On the return journey, the portion from Leeds had to wait again for up to ten minutes at Low Moor while the portion from Bradford arrived in the adjacent platform and was then drawn out of the station before being shunted back to the head the portion from Leeds, and the journey was eventually resumed.

This complicated operation ceased with the introduction of diesel multiple units – the train went straight into Bradford and the driver would simply walk from one end to the other to drive it out to Leeds – as still happens today.

The exchange station at Bradford was a huge barn of a place – ten platforms, with an overall roof based on the design of the original St Pancras in London (before Eurostar took it over). I used to enjoy exploring the nooks and crannies of Bradford's magnificent station, particularly the refreshment room in the corner where you could purchase a glass of orange juice for 6d and a Lyon's Individual Fruit Pie for 1s.6d. This was a treat. Coming in its own box, it measured about 4" x 4" with lovely pastry and a crust coated with sugar on top and a filling of various assortments of fruit – apple, raspberry, etc.

There was also an interesting machine on the platform, red and about 4ft high, resembling an early dymo tape printing machine, but using thin metal strips rather than plastic tape. It had a big pointer on the front like a clock face and a handle at the side. For 2d or so, you could print your nametag on a strip of metal by using the pointer to select the letters, before embossing the letter on to the tape by pressing down the handle at the side. Great fun, and no trip to Bradford was complete without returning with a freshly printed name tag!

(However my happy memories of these machines were rather darkened when I later read somewhere that such machines had often been used by infantry embarking on their journeys to the Somme and other battlefields, to provided some kind of identification were they to be slain in action.)

The climax of the journey to Bradford was the return. By choosing a heavy train of more than three coaches, you could be rewarded with the glorious sounds of being banked up the steep gradient out of Bradford to Bowling. The engine which brought the stock into the station, would uncouple from the train, but push with all its worth while the engine at the front pulled it up the bank, until they both reached the summit at Bowling, where the banker would drop off, ready to be crossed over and run back down to Bradford.

If I chose to go instead to Leeds, there were other delights awaiting after what seemed an interminable wait at Low Moor for the shunting to take place. The run to Leeds Central would be speedy.

At that stage, Leeds had two stations – Central and City, with a walk of about half a mile between the two. A visit to Leeds City station offered a much larger railway scene, with trains from the old Midland and North Eastern lines to observe. There was also at City what was known then as a 'News Theatre'. Intended for people with an hour or so to spare between trains, it showed a continuous programme of cartoons and newsreels, and you entered and left as you wished. The rolling news was the forerunner of what we have on TV today, but the number of Tom and Jerry cartoons I saw there! And if I didn't fancy City Station and cartoons, there were the Leeds City Tramways to explore.

These were not the modern trams winding through the streets of Manchester or Sheffield as of today, but the old double-deck 70-seaters with little suspension, clanking their way to suburbs such as Roundhay or Cross Gates, with the conductor reversing the seat-backs at the terminus and swinging the trolley from front to back with a bamboo pole. A bit like the scene at Crich Tramway museum today, but in Leeds, for real, in the late 1950s–early 60s.

Journeys to Bradford, Leeds or Manchester on the main line would afford me comfortable, corridor stock with compartments for six and large windows to admire the view. However, if I chose to go towards Huddersfield or Penistone on the branch, it was usually non-corridor stock – three coaches of narrow compartments seating six or so per side and an individual door at each end with an opening window you released with a leather strap, rather like a barber's strop.

The bench seats were upholstered (if that's the right word), with a rough horsehair fabric, long lasting but very prickly on the legs of a short-trousered boy. They were also far from clean. Even just to place your hand on the bench next to you resulted in great clouds of dust rising into the atmosphere. To clear the dust you opened the window, only to be then assailed by smoke and smut from the firebox of the engine in front. Oh, the luxuries of train travel in those days!

The journey up the branch to Penistone was worth it though, for once I had cleared the town of Huddersfield, I entered the beautiful area of what is popularly known as 'The Last of the Summer Wine' country today. We called at sleepy little wayside halts such as Stocksmoor, Shepley & Shelley and Denby Dale & Cumberworth. Penistone was a bleak settlement out on the moors and you might wonder why I would go there, but then my route met up with the famous Woodhead Line from Manchester, where a magnificent EM2 DC electric loco would whisk me in modern coaches down to Sheffield Victoria in fifteen minutes or so.

Originating at the then Manchester London Rd station, the line used the Woodhead tunnel to reach Sheffield, and with a change if engine, expresses continued via the Great Central Railway to London Marylebone. Closed to passengers in 1970, it is still greatly missed and mourned by rail enthusiasts today. Imagine alighting from dirty L&Y train at a windswept Penistone station to await a sleek electric loco – one of a batch named *Electra, Ariande, Aurora, Juno, Minerva* or *Pandora* … They were a wonderful introduction to Greek Mythology for the enquiring mind. The Railway of the Future, we thought in the 1960's. Little did we know.

So why did they insist on dragging me round Leeds on a shopping expedition? At least my Uncle Laurie, Auntie Lottie and Granny Jackson seem to be enjoying themselves. Note the Yorkshire Woollen District bus in the background

Chapter 8

Planning for the Future

Another growing interest, which was to play a huge part in my future life, was the church. I suppose it should have come as no surprise to me that my love of railways went hand-in-hand with the church, as exemplified in such authors as the late Bishop Eric Treacy with his spectacular photography, the Revd W H Audrey, the Revd 'Teddy' Boston, and several others.

In the early 1960s, the village of Copley near my childhood home welcomed a new vicar – a Revd Eric Davis. He had worked in engineering before being trained at Lichfield for ordination, and served his curacy in Haworth. St. Stephen's, Copley was his first sole charge and he must have been about 40 years old when he arrived. He was a friendly, unassuming man with neither edge nor car, so he walked around the parish and stopped to chat with everyone he met. You could do that in those far gone days of 'one man-one parish'. And it was a traditional parish, with little lay-leadership and where the vicar did most things from preaching on the Sunday to turning on the boiler on Saturday night.

Every Sunday evening, the churchwardens would count the collection, bag it and enter the totals in the book, and then give it to him to bank the following day. I think the Revd Eric secretly liked this, as it gave him the excuse to get the bus into town each Monday morning, with his bag of 'swank' in his coat pocket (usually no more than £5 in small change). He would visit the bank and then repair to one of the growing number of coffee bars before returning home. He might have even declared the coffee on his expenses!

And he talked to everyone on the bus, including my mother. One day she came home, excited by the news she'd met the New Vicar and he'd talked to her, and he was just a 'normal human being' – something I'm afraid his predecessor was not overly successful at conveying.

Revd Eric had told her that attendance figures were pretty low and he was worried about this, and when this news was relayed to me and my father, we all decided to go along the following Sunday night to 'cheer him up!' (Yes, really!).

To be fair, it wasn't a total change of heart on our part – my mother was nominal C of E and had bothered sufficiently to have me baptised into it some twelve years earlier, and my father, coming from Gorseinon, was originally a Welsh Independent Methodist. He enjoyed giving rip to such hymns as *Blaenwern* and *Cwm Rhondda,* but was rather bored by the versicles, psalms and Cranmerian English of the first part of Evensong. My baptism must have eventually worked upon me, and well done the Revd Eric Davis, for carefully drawing it back out of us. So we became regular attenders at Evensong, and virtually doubled the congregation.

Being a traditional parish priest and having the luxury of just one small parish, Eric placed much faith in pastoral visiting, and would frequently visit us on a Monday night. Now perish the thought that the fact he had no TV in his vicarage (but he loved Western films and there was often one on at 8pm on a Monday) had anything to do with it.

But often there would be a knock at 7.55pm, and with a 'Don't switch it off, Taff', he would settle down with a cup of tea until it ended at 10pm. Then he'd get up and go, often forgetting what, if anything, he'd come to see us about.

However, one night after the film he was grave.

'I've got the Bishop coming next Sunday for a Confirmation, and I've no candidates,' he announced.

Quick as a flash, my father and I said, 'We'll be

confirmed', as we didn't want to let the side down and have him look unsuccessful in the eyes of the Bishop.

So, with minimal preparation, we had episcopal hands laid upon us at 3pm the following Sunday by Dr John Ramsbotham, by the Grace of God Lord Bishop of Wakefield.

I often thought of this episode in my future ministry when I stressed the importance of self-examination and careful consideration, followed by at least 3 months of preparation before presenting any of my parishioners to the Bishop for this sacrament. (Hypocrite? Me?)

From then on, I played a growing part in church life, joining the choir, serving at Communion and regularly reading lessons. I was quite nervous doing this, and always tried to prepare carefully beforehand. I still remember vividly the day when the second lesson was about Peter in the Courtyard of the High Priest after Jesus had been arrested.

The scriptures recall that Peter was warming his hands on a brazier, as the servant girls came up and accused him of being a follower of Jesus. Alarm bells started to ring in my mind as I prepared this lesson beforehand, but as usual, the more aware of the pitfalls you are the more nervous you become and the more likely you are to fall into them. Sure enough, come the night, I stood there and solemnly read that Peter warmed his hands, but gave the source of heat a short 'a' instead of a long one …

'It's good to tell Stuart's got a girlfriend,' someone observed after the service.

And the mind boggles at the thought of Peter, standing there, warming his hands on a —.

After a while, the inevitable question 'What are you going to do if you grow up?' began to surface.

My father wanted me to be a schoolmaster. He'd been influenced either by someone he respected in the Welsh Valleys, or more likely, by the 1939 film *Goodbye Mr Chips* starring Robert Donat, Greer Garson and John Mills, based on the novel by James Hilton.

I, however, was beginning to feel the tug towards the church. This didn't go away, and I eventually experienced what must be the shortest meeting on record with the school's career master, who, having learned what I felt I wanted to do, stood-up, shook my hand and said 'Do let us know how you get on.' And that was it.

Fortunately Eric Davis's successor as Vicar of Copley, the Revd Brian Cole, supported me and sent me off to the Fellowship of Vocation afternoons the diocese of Wakefield was then running. This process consisted of attending endless garden parties, and talking to various diocesan dignitaries about how you felt, and meeting with the Diocesan Director of Vocations.

The strategy on discerning vocations at that time seemed to be listen to the potential ordinand and then send him/her away to return in 6 month's time. After repeating this cycle a further two times, if you still felt a nagging call after all that, you were sent off to see the Bishop for his inspection.

My Bishop at the time was the Rt Revd Eric Treacy, well known as a steam engine enthusiast, who had published several excellent books of photographs of steam locomotives at work, who put me through a most rigorous examination of my faith and suitability, as we talked about Black Fives, Jubilees, steam engines, Yorkshire branch lines, steam engines, railwaymen, and did I mention steam engines?

In the meanwhile I'd somehow managed to scrape together 9 'O' levels and between the 5th and 6th years I held my first holiday job. This, in the summer of 1965, entailed helping with a traffic census in Halifax. The planners were busily trying to predict the future road systems that would be necessary to cope with the growing number of cars and lorries which would be passing through the town. This eventually led to the building of the bypass to carry the A58 traffic around the town centre and away towards Leeds and Bradford by a new impressive viaduct spanning the River Hebble brook, which opened in 1982.

Those of us who were recording the census were paired up into twos, and we spent hours at a time gathered in shop doorways in an attempt to escape from the Northern summer – ie driving rain, with clipboards and hand held tally counters, one for lorries, one for cars, one for busses, etc, in an attempt to record the traffic situation at the time. When we'd mastered the art of clicking the counter, and it didn't take too long (for, remember, we were potential 6th formers at the local grammar school), we were promoted to interviewing drivers.

The police would divert a batch of cars, the number corresponding with the number of interviewers available, into a coned off lay-by. We would then approach the drivers, armed with a bunch of pens, stacks of questionnaires and buckets of hope that they would wind down their windows and happily answer our questions; such as where did they start their journey, where were they going, what was the purpose of their journey, what was their shoe size?, etc.

This proved to be valuable experience for my later ministry in dealing with members of the public, for some drivers were co-operative and seemed to appreciate the opportunity to take a break and relate their life story to a total stranger; others were less forthcoming, particularly concerning where they had come from as they didn't want to reveal where they'd spent the previous night (even though we didn't ask with whom). A few preferred to exercise their right of silence by simply gesticulating through the glass that they wished we'd go away, as they only had two more miles to their destination.

We had been told to simply walk away in that situation and avoid any conflict, but it did amuse me somewhat when, having sent me away, the driver then realised he could not escape out of the lay-by because the exit was blocked by drivers in front happily chatting away helping other interviewers to the full.

Now, whenever I return to visit Halifax, it always gives me a great sense of pride to gaze at the traffic chaos, hold my head high, and think 'I was responsible for organising some of that'.

With a happy Mother, having escaped from Sutcliffe
Buildings back to Skircoat Green, c.1957

*Same site, but without the Mother. Gained a
jacket, but not quite learned to stand independently*

Chapter 9

Finishing School

I started the 6th form as a prefect, studying English Literature, Geography and General Studies, and still with a nagging feeling I wanted to be a parish priest. Regarding discipline, I suppose I was rather pragmatic, preferring to reason with someone rather than place them on detention (particularly as you had to stay behind with them to supervise it).

Brian Cole, then Vicar of Copley, tried to further my vocation by getting me my next holiday job as porter at Halifax General Hospital, where he was also chaplain, as it was then becoming obvious that Copley was too small a parish to support a full-time priest.

Looking back, I think being a hospital porter was one of the most rewarding holiday jobs I had. My role was to transport the quick and the dead – the quick from the ward to x-ray, which, in those days, was out in a hut across the cobbled courtyard, and the dead from the ward to the mortuary, which was in another hut across the same cobbled courtyard, but woe betide you if you confused the two.

The latter was a job calling for great sensitivity. You'd find a colleague, and together change into your best white smock, and collect a metal enclosed trolley with a white cloth and a vase of flowers on it. Passageways were cleared in advance for you and you were allowed to reserve the lift by leaving the doors open – the only time you could get away with this without incurring the wrath of other porters. You arrived at the ward by appointment, and found the lights dimmed and the screens pulled around all the beds, forming a direct channel a bit like the parting of the Red Sea, down the central aisle to the bed which was your destination. You were in and out within a few minutes, Then with screens taken away and lights restored, life on the ward continued as though nothing had happened.

Such was the attitude to death in those days, but the long-stay patients soon learned to look round to see who wasn't there compared with half an hour or so before.

Another job which fell to the porters was working the hospital switchboard during the lunch break, when the regular operator had her meal. I enjoyed that immensely — the wires, the plugs, the headphones, the power, connecting outside lines to the various wards and departments. Young women would ring and ask 'Can you put me on to Maternity?' and you resisted the temptation to reply 'With pleasure', substituting the more usual phrase, 'Trying to connect you'.

Towards the end of my school years, the diocese still hadn't decided whether the C of E was facing enough problems without having me on the payroll, so I opted to study theology, thinking if the church decided she could do without me, I could still use it to teach. So when UCCA time arrived, I chose Leeds University, Lampeter Theological College and King's College London. Amazingly I was invited to interview at all three.

The journey to Leeds was easy – being just a forty minute train ride away, and I was offered a place on condition of gaining my 3 'A' levels. The journey from Halifax to London was interesting – train to Kings Cross then bus to the Strand, where the then Dean the Revd Sidney Hall Evans, offered me a place to study for the Associateship of Kings College (AKC), again on provision of my achieving satisfactory 'A' level results.

The expedition to Lampeter was more challenging. This involved catching a train to Manchester Victoria, walking across the city to Manchester Piccadilly to catch another train to Crewe and then to Shrewsbury, where I connected with my final train, the named *Cambrian*

Coast Express to Aberystwyth. This 'express' had been delayed on its journey north from London Paddington and departed Shrewsbury about 1 hour late to chug gently along the Cambrian, through Welshpool and over Talerdigg summit to Machynlleth, eventually arriving at a desolate Aberystwyth ninety or so minutes late. The last bus connections had long gone.

But here, a railway porter took pity on me and offered a lift in his Austin A30 to Lampeter, claiming it was 'on his way home' although I did wonder just where he lived if this was his route. Of course, in those days safeguarding was unheard of, and I gratefully accepted the ride in a stranger's car, arriving in Lampeter at about 7pm, just too late for dinner, and dined on a packet of crisps before bedding down for the night.

My interview was first-up at 9.30am the following morning, and I was aware I had to catch the 10.30 bus back to Aberystwyth to get back to Halifax the same day. Understandably I did not give my best interview. I left feeling I didn't really care if I never went there again, and was not unduly disappointed to hear a week or so later that I was not accepted. But it was all grist to the mill, and I marvel that many years later, I am now proud to have a stepdaughter, an intelligent and highly gifted author-artist, who has made a much greater success of an Aberystwyth education than I ever did.

So – Leeds or Kings London were my offers. My father decided it abruptly by forbidding me to accept Leeds, as it was only an hour or so away, and in effect I'd never leave home.

I was admitted through the hallowed portals of Kings College London in the autumn of 1967. My father had wisely said that if I were going to leave home then go early on the appointed day so they wouldn't be waiting around like a dog's dinner for me to leave, so I caught the 6.30am train from Halifax and was in London Kings Cross by 10.30am, a mere 7½ hours before I was expected at Halliday Hall on Clapham Common South Side at 6pm.

I was very lucky in getting a room at Halliday Hall. It was situated almost opposite the Windmill Pub on Clapham Common, and had been a hotel in its earlier days. It had a ballroom, an extensive rose garden, tennis courts and a bar with snooker room, and some of its rooms even had en-suite facilities. You were expected to dress for dinner at 7pm, followed by coffee in the drawing room, where the Warden insisted on pouring the coffee into tiny cups personally, and having a chat with all the residents.

I shared a double room for the first year, but had it to myself at weekends as my room-mate was a love-sick individual from Reading who insisted on going home to his girlfriend as often as possible. Eventually, he just forgot to return.

Being a hostel for all Kings College students and not just those feeling called to the church, Halliday Hall gave ample opportunity to debate amongst, play croquet against and sup with those of all disciplines. Only on hearing later of the hovels some students had to face, with uncaring private landlords, faulty gas boilers and damp, dirty rooms, did I realise just how fortunate I had been.

Up for a cooked breakfast at 8am, a gentle stroll down to Clapham Common tube station, a ride on the Northern Line to Embankment and a walk to Kings College for 10am. Then return at teatime, a bath, dinner at 7pm, a little studying before a nightcap in the bar and possibly a game of snooker before retiring for the night. I seem to remember I adapted to this lifestyle quite easily. Life was good.

Chapter 10

Studying Theology

The Theological Faculty of Kings London took a very radical approach – in the real sense of delving back into the roots of belief. This was no bad thing for a person who'd come up from a protected background, and had accepted everything the local vicar said as 'gospel'. All I knew was that every word in the Bible was true (and therefore accepted that Jesus must have had a faithful team of secretaries, some working for Matthew, others Mark, some for Luke and a few for John, following behind in shifts, recording his every word, thought and action. Even in the wilderness, when he thought he was alone with the wild beasts, there must have been one or two hiding behind the nearest boulder, pens at the ready, out of sight but well within hearing range …)

It came as quite a surprise to discover that the earliest account of Jesus was not recorded until AD 64, some 30 or so years after the event. So, at Kings, the key to unlocking the gospels was 'form-criticism'. I was taught to study the events to discover earlier oral traditions – legends, folktales, parables and myths etc. I learned that a 'myth' is not a lie as in the popular sense, but a story which conveys theological truth but may not have any historical basis. And having discerned the possible original source of the story, I proceeded to try to see it in its sociological setting – its 'sitz-im-Leben' or setting in life – and to understand that it had then been used by the evangelist to contribute to their text as a whole, and the impression they were seeking to portray.

That's the *Idiot's Guide to Form-Criticism,* and I apologise for its over-simplification – should any reader wish to know more, consult the many books which have been written on the subject. But you can hopefully see how this approach led to the familiar cry of many a first year Kings student – 'they've taken away my faith'. Fortunately most found it returned even more strongly as the year progressed.

The Kings strategy also included learning the language in which the gospels were first written, ie New Testament Greek, which was different from Classical Greek and a world apart again from modern Greek. A lot for a lad from up North to get his head round.

We did enjoy some excellent lecturers, and, apologies

to the rest if I mention here just two – Dr Eric Mascall, who was professor of Historical Theology (he was the only lecturer to receive a standing ovation after every session); and Canon Ronald Jasper, lecturer in liturgical studies, who gave us a deeper knowledge into what was said and done and where in the various prayer books and orders of service, such as Matins or Holy Communion, and why it was said at all.

In my future early ministry, the Church's introduction of the *Alternative Service Book* was accompanied by much grumbling in the pews along the lines of 'why can't the church leave things alone? After all if 16th century Cranmerian orders were good enough for Jesus himself, then surely we didn't have to meddle with them?', but it was interesting to me to know that this change was actually an attempt to rediscover the earlier forms of service, going back to well before Cranmer.

The whole faculty was overseen by the Dean, Canon Sydney Hall Evans, who was an influential churchman of the time, and well known as a pastor and nurturer of potential who sought to offer a University education to those who otherwise might not have had the chance, but who did not suffer fools gladly. He personally interviewed you in depth at the end of each term, assessing your progress, and was not slow to tell you that you need not return next term if he felt you were found wanting. But, wielding even more power than that was his secretary, Miss Winifred Medway. Like any good secretary should, she protected her boss in his inner sanctum, and it was said that it was easier to gain an audience with the Pope than get past her desk.

In those days before texts, emails, mobile phones etc, the only way her office could contact you quickly was for her to chalk your name up on the board outside, and you were instructed to walk past that board at least once a day to check your name was not inscribed thereon. If it was, you certainly popped into the chapel first to pray for divine protection, for I saw not only youthful students but mature men cower before her. One day someone noticed an article in a local Kent newspaper about a person being pulled out of the river near Rochester by the emergency services, and posted the headline on the board, presumably in the early hours while no one was around, and then made a quick escape. The headline read in large letters 'Police rescue student from Medway!' It was much appreciated by those who crept by, and the fact it stayed up for the whole day led me to think that Miss Medway enjoyed it too.

During my first Christmas break, I was again summoned to Bishop's Lodge in Wakefield, to be informed the diocese had decided 'What the heck, it can't get any worse' and they would take a chance on sponsoring me for ordination.

This meant that I would go before a selection conference, arranged by what was called in those days CACTM – the Church's Advisory Council for the Training of Candidates for the Ministry. This august body has undergone several changes of name and approach since then, but in my time it had a very rigorous set up and was based on selection methods used by the armed services – I suppose that was then the only model the church knew, although there was of course a bit of a difference between being selected to be a Brigadier General and a pastor in the church.

There was a standard format – assemble on a Friday afternoon, be observed, examined and interviewed throughout the weekend. It was even rumoured that they observed whether you used the right cutlery at dinner. You then had to lead a service of worship on the Sunday, before departing on the Monday morning, leaving your selectors and inquisitors debating your future life.

You were questioned on your faith, your academic ability, your personal life, and there was also a lay-man or woman who examined you from the point of view of could they stand you as their Vicar? It afforded little recognition of the prophetic aspect of ministry – pleasing the laity was what it was all about – after all, they and the dead paid your stipend by parish share and legacy. My conference was at Greyladies Retreat House, Blackheath. I think it is now holiday lettings. Then it was as far removed from a holiday as possible.

A week or so later, I was again summoned to Bishop's Lodge to be told I was accepted for training on condition I did some secular employment between finishing studying and ordination. That was no problem, as, having gone straight from school to University to Theological College, I would have to wait from Trinity Sunday of 1971 to Michaelmas, as the lower age limit for ordination was then 23, and my birthday was not until September.

My acceptance for ordination training meant I had to leave the comfortable Halliday Hall for my third year, and reside in Kings College Hostel, Vincent Square. This was quite a shock to the system, for it was back to single rooms with toilets and communal bathing at the end of the corridor.

In place of the dining room we had the refectory, and the monastic similarity was also continued in the fact there was no genial conversation during meals. Rather these were held in silence, while someone read highly improving and enlightening texts from a lectern.

In place of the ballroom was the chapel, where

attendance for Matins and Holy Communion every morning was mandatory. You also searched in vain for the bar! Guests were allowed only between the hours of 2pm and 9pm, and had to be signed in and out, and if the latter hadn't been done by 9.05pm, the heavy banging on the door was the porter enquiring why not. I sometimes wondered what it was you could enjoy with your guest in the privacy of your room between 2–9pm, but which was strictly forbidden after 9pm and 2pm the following day. You could always go out for the evening, but the curfew was at 10pm – after which the heavy doors were locked and a night on a bench in St James's Park was the alternative (provided you were back, washed and in your place in chapel for 7.40am!)

Ironically, I met Madeleine – a geology student – during this year when I might have appreciated more the opportunity to entertain her, but our feelings did grow and we eventually married in 1974.

Another memory of the hostel involves the feeding arrangements on a Sunday. Then lunch was served in the refectory at 1pm, after which the door was locked and the cook awarded the rest of the day off. So after lunch you collected a brown paper bag, containing a pork pie, an apple and a bag of crisps. That was supposed to sustain a growing man until 8.30am on the following morning. But when one door closes, another opens, and this one, wide open to most hostel students on a Sunday evening was, if I remember its correct title, the Shah-Noor Indian Restaurant on nearby Rochester Row.

Here, my theological education was completed with the discovery of such delights as chicken korma or beef jalfrezi. On returning home at Christmas and hearing I was enjoying Indian food, my mother was initially shocked (this was 1969), but then tried to accommodate my taste by purchasing one of those early easy-cook Indian curries – a meagre portion of plain white rice and some unappetising curry powder containing bits of dried meat, reconstituted by adding water and heat – which, despite her best efforts, wasn't quite the same.

These days, I see now that the hostel is enjoying a new life as the 4 star Grange Wellington Hotel, where a high quality double room will set you back £189 per night. The only thing I recognise through the photos on the website are the heraldic shields in the stained glass windows of what was the refectory. There's no sign of the chapel of course – perhaps it was the room now converted to the gym with all its awesome-looking fitness machines. If clergy were still trained here, they'd be the slimmest priests around.

Surprisingly, my 9 months spent there passed quite

quickly and I managed to become an Associate of King's College in the summer of 1970. Remembering my selection conference's recommendations, I expected to take a year out to learn a bit more about how the real world works, but I think my superiors took my experience of counting cars (dealing with some abrupt drivers) and hospital portering into account, and sent me immediately for my 4th year of training at St. Augustine's College, Canterbury, starting in September 1970.

A nice, peaceful Summer Sunday afternoon with my parents in the grounds of Manor Heath, Halifax

Chapter 11

Canterbury

In Southwerk at the Tabard as I lay
Redy to wenden on my pilgrimage
To Caunterbury with ful devout corage
At nyght was come into that hostelrye
Wel nyne and twenty in a compaignye
Of sondry folk, by aventure yfalle
In felaweshipe, and pilgrims were they alle,
That toward Caunterbury wolden ryde.

The Canterbury Tales by **Geoffrey Chaucer**

Well, with due apologies to Geoffrey Chaucer, it was not in the Southwark tavern but at Charing Cross station where I began my pilgrimage. Nevertheless, I was not lacking in ful devout corage as I gathered in a sort of felaweshipe with other pilgrims/ passengers intent on riding to that city, not on horseback but in the comfort of the electric multiple, two 4-Vcp units forming the 2pm departure.

We steadily passed through the south London suburbs, and once clear of Orpington, we raced down Knockholt bank, safely round the bend to Tonbridge and then fair galloped along the final straight to Ashford. There, we paused for a few minutes before continuing to Canterbury West, winding through the charming Kentish villages of Wye, Chilham and Chartham on the way – or as someone once misheard the station announcer proclaiming, 'Why kill 'em and cart 'em to Canterbury?'

Why indeed. And the journey was so swift we had hardly the time to greet our fellow pilgrims let alone relate them tales, and I never got to meet the wife of Bath.

St Augustine's Abbey, my new home, had experienced a chequered history. It was a Benedictine monastery founded in 598 and functioned as such a monastery until its dissolution in 1538 during the English Reformation. By the 16th century, it had, according to Robert Ewell's *Guide to St Augustines Abbey*:

> '…*reached its lowest point of degradation. The gate was the entrance to a brewery, the kitchin was a public house and the grounds were used for dancing and fireworks.*'

After the abbey's dissolution, it underwent dismantlement, but in 1848, it was rebuilt as a Missionary College, as part of the mass-migration from England to its colonies. The C of E had sent clergy, but demand exceeded supply, hence the need for increasing available training facilities. The buildings included a large undercroft beneath the library, which had originally been intended for the teaching of practical skills such as woodwork – invaluable to the clergy when they reached their colonial parishes, and probably had to play a large part in building their own churches.

In my time, that was reduced to simply a large space, useful instead for drama and liturgical experimentation. Which is just as well, as I very much doubt the good folk of my first parish, Golcar, had much need of wonky teapot stands. What was left of the abbey ruins were preserved for their historical value.

By the time I knew St Augustine's Abbey, it was no longer a Missionary College. Between the years 1952–67, it had held the Central College of the Anglican Communion, with its purpose neatly reversed, for as a Missionary College, its focus had been on training clergy for work overseas – now it brought clergy and students from throughout the world back to Canterbury, for further study together. They often brought examples of their own indigenous liturgies with them, and it must have been a very interesting place.

When that closed in 1967, it took on the form that I experienced – its final role was to provide 4th year training in practical theology for ordinands from Kings College, a role it occupied until 1976, when the site was then adopted by the independent boarding school The Kings School, Canterbury.

So I began my fourth year of study at St Augustine's Abbey. As its purpose suggests, it was supposed to give me practical training for when I would be let loose on an unsuspecting parish for my first curacy. This was more difficult than it sounds, for it was hard to emulate parish conditions and situations in isolation in a rarefied college atmosphere. For example, we practised conducting Baptism services using a rubber doll (yes!), and it was difficult to simulate a parish situation around the font with coo-ing mothers, uncertain and embarrassed godparents and noisy children rushing round the church, when in reality you were surrounded by giggling students, scoring you out of 10 and hoping you'd make a mess of it.

Also, very importantly, you had to remember that a real baby did not bounce if accidentally dropped on the stone church floor. Having said that, if that doll still survives somewhere, it's the holiest doll in Christendom.

Incidentally, this state of affairs led to one of the tensions when we were finally let loose on a parish. The regulars there were looking forward to someone straight out of college, with fresh ideas and new bright solutions to the ongoing problems. What they received was a well-meaning, but unsure person, with everything to learn.

We were farmed out to certain parishes in the area to learn practical skills there, but again this was of limited use. I was sent with three others every Wednesday and Thursday afternoon to Whitstable Parish Church, and attended the team meetings between the elderly Canon and his frustrated new curate. This seemed to consist mainly of the Canon drawing up the rotas for the coming week, and the curate making the tea for us all. Obviously the Canon did not have a wife … (only joking!)

We were asked to preach once a month – usually at Evensong, where the congregation was smaller (and more long-suffering!). When it was my turn, it was the role of the other three members of my team to support me by sitting in the front pews and pulling funny faces, or shake and tap their watches every minute or so. And if I was lucky, they did both. Then my efforts were marked the following morning.

But let's be positive about my time at St Augustine's. We did a course on group dynamics, which came in very useful later for discovering what was really going on at PCCs (Parochial Church Council Meetings) and clergy chapter meetings. We also did the Myers-Briggs Indicator course to identify our personality type. I forget my full results, but remember I was deeply in the 'introverted' sector. Interestingly, many clergy were accordingly deemed introverted, and these were people who were supposed to lead the PCCs out of despair, heartily welcome newcomers of all shapes and sizes into the parish and be the life and soul of the Harvest Supper. We had to embrace being a discreet and sensitive counsellor to the needy and troubled, and then give the impression that announcing the winning raffle numbers at the annual fete was the most fulfilling thing we had ever been asked to do – an event that was a source of further conflict in the parish!

We also had a fantastic library of which to avail ourselves, and being only a stone's throw away from Canterbury Cathedral meant we had stirring and thought provoking preachers on our doorstep. College life was more relaxed – the large wooden gates of the gatehouse were closed at 7pm, but if you were going to be out late you simply borrowed a key for the small gate round the corner. Very biblical that – enter by the narrow gate, and good advice too, unless you were accompanied by your camel.

Guests were not frowned upon, and Madeleine spent one or two weekends with me – not in my room of course, but the college owned six small cottages just outside the college grounds which were intended for married couples with children, and one couple yet to start a family kindly allowed her to stay in their spare room.

And on another positive note, feeling that I should become acquainted with Kent in all aspects, I discovered the excellent Shepherd Neame brewery in nearby Faversham, and developed a taste for a pint of Spitfire or Bishop's Finger to accompany my games of bar-billiards in the local around the corner.

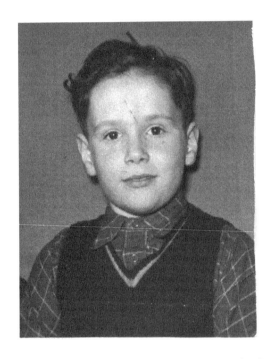

*School photograph from Copley Primary School
c.1958. Angelic looks marred by scar on forehead
(which remains with me to this day) caused by
unexpected projection over handlebars into the
sharp 90 degree edge of a stone pillar, caused by
front small wheel of my pedal scooter getting caught
on uneven paving stones, resulting in much blood,
crying, frantic parents, a taxi-ride to Halifax Royal
Infirmary and 6 stitches.*

*The stone pillar, the neighbour was pleased to
discover, was undamaged*

Chapter 12

Easter at Canterbury

The liturgical highlight of St Augustine's was staying over Holy Week and Easter, as we did not go home for the holiday until Easter Morning. This enabled us to celebrate all the Holy Week Services, the full Maundy Thursday and Good Friday rites, and most importantly, the Dawn Mass of Easter, starting at 4.30am on Easter Day in the grounds of the Abbey ruins.

It was still cloudy and chilly as we assembled, wondering why ever we'd risen from our warm beds. But by the time we got to the reading of the Easter gospel, the sun was beginning to rise and some warmth return. A truly invigorating spiritual experience.

After the service we trooped into the refectory, full of Easter joy, for a hearty breakfast, before leaving for home, and found someone had decided to revive the old tradition, abolished at the Reformation, of lighting celebratory fireworks, waking up most of Canterbury as a result.

I returned after the Easter break for the final term with the news that the diocese had decided to allocate to me the parish of Golcar for my Assistant Curacy. I'd visited a couple of times during the holiday, met the vicar and felt I was called to the place. It was a working class parish then of about 12,000 people, about three miles out of Huddersfield along the northern slopes of the Colne Valley.

There were mills and other industries in the valley bottom near the source of the water, and housing up the hillside, reaching to the farms of Bolster Moor and Scapegoat Hill at the top. I seemed to be forever going uphill or downhill. The parish church was dedicated to St John the Evangelist, and was situated in the centre of the village on Town End. There was also a small Mission church at Westwood, out on the hills overlooking Slaithwaite. The vicar, and so my future boss, was John Mowll, a very saintly and kind man, and a great teacher. He'd neither married nor learned to drive, had very few practical skills, and was struggling to pastor that village in his older age, relying upon his housekeeper to feed him, and the local bus drivers or parishioners with cars to get him around.

Shortly after my appointment had been announced, a very charitable mill owner, who was churchwarden and organist at the Mission Church, decided to provide a car and insurance for the use of the vicar and myself. That raised a small problem in that I couldn't drive – my family never having had enough money to run to such a luxury – so I returned to Canterbury after the Easter break and took a course of driving lessons. These were then £1 a time, and I think I had six or seven, supplemented by the help of a friend who owned a small car and sat in with me as I practised driving in between lessons.

I thoroughly enjoyed myself driving round the Kent countryside in either the British School of Motoring's dark green Austin 1100 or my friend's grey Morris Minor.

I took my test in the centre of Canterbury on a Friday teatime at 3.30pm on a hot day in June. The traffic was beginning to build up (there was neither ringroad nor M2 in those days), and I eventually became firmly stuck – the car in a massive traffic jam, and me to the driver's seat by my shirt as I was perspiring heavily.

I'd like to report the examiner was cool and collected, but I can't really. Rather he shifted uncomfortably in the passenger seat, holding his clipboard and looking anxiously at his watch every minute or so, as he had another test to conduct. For my part, I was convinced I'd failed, so just relaxed and enjoyed the view, as there was nothing more I could do about it other than inch forward as the occasion allowed, and we eventually arrived back at the test centre about 40 minutes late, whereupon my examiner handed me the appropriate piece of paper and leapt out to the next awaiting candidate, leaving me with the sweetest words 'Congratulations – you've passed.'

To crown it all, my mill owner was true to his word and I officially arrived in Golcar after my ordination that September to be met by a reception party including the vicar and his housekeeper, one or two amused parishioners and a red VW Beetle – registration WHE 926J – there. I still remember it.

Looking back I enjoyed my time in London and Canterbury, and am always grateful to the tax-payers of West Yorkshire, for I received a grant for the whole of my 4 year's course.

Chapter 13

New Beginnings

Madeleine and I celebrated the ending of my course at Canterbury with a holiday in North Devon. We caught a train to Taunton and then a bus to Minehead, where we stayed the night. The following day we boarded one of the few Southern National buses to Lynmouth – a fantastic scenic ride through Porlock, up Porlock Hill, across Exmoor and down Countisbury Hill to Lynmouth. I was enraptured by the scenery.

Madeleine had enjoyed holidays in North Devon before when her mother was still alive – for me, this was my first time I'd visited. We stayed in a B&B along the road to the Watersmeet and walked all around the area, discovering Brendon, Parracombe and Heddon's Mouth. We eventually bought a little cottage in Parracombe, and enjoyed many happy times there until her untimely death from cancer in 1996.

Travelling in those days was quite an experience

concerning management of money. Strange as it may seem to relate now, I was the first member of the Samuel family to hold a bank account. My parents had some savings in the Building Society as they'd continued paying in after paying off the mortgage of £1560 on the house they bought in 1957. For the rest, my father duly handed over the £20 or so he earned every Friday, and Mother split the money into so much for the electricity, so much for food and provisions, etc, and so much for pocket money, into various tins and containers, and that's the way the economy of the Samuel family worked. If they needed to send a sum of money anywhere, for example paying for our first family holiday in Rhyl, it was down to the Post Office to purchase a postal order and a stamp. For me, it all changed when I went to university and received a grant cheque – I had to open a bank account.

In those days with no debit cards, cash machines, internet banking, banks were keen to separate you from your money as much as possible, issuing you with simply a cheque book and a paying-in book. You could only draw money from your account by cheque at your home branch, and if you were likely to want to obtain cash elsewhere, you had to name that place in advance at your home bank, saying how much you expected to want to withdraw per week, and give a specimen signature.

That was then posted to the branch where you would be staying.

So I would arrive at the hallowed counter of the branch in Lynton, and beg them to let me have some of my money.

'Have you got an arrangement?' would be the response of the cashier, looking down his or her nose at me. Upon receiving my timid affirmation, a clerk would be sent into the back room to check my signature with that on record, and eventually they would reluctantly part with the £5 or so, giving the impression they believed it was being taken from their week's wages.

On my return home from our trip to Devon, I got my final holiday job as Care Assistant in a residential home in Halifax. This mainly involved washing, shaving, dusting and dressing the elderly men and checking they were eating properly. The more alert ones provided a certain amount of banter, and I remember being regarded most suspiciously and subjected to much ridicule by one obnoxious gentleman when he found out I was waiting to be ordained.

Every day I put up with his scornful comments until the day I left, when he presented me with a tatted cross he'd made himself and wished me well.

That gift meant so much. I still have it, and for me, the popular hymn should read not 'I cling to the old Rugged Cross', but the old Tatted Cross.

Note: 'tatting' is a process of knotting string or thread into lace

Chapter 14

Ordination

Ordination in the C of E was a twofold process in 1971. Firstly, you were made deacon then after a year you were ordained priest. In times gone by, the office of deacon, or the diaconate, was an ancient order of those who served in the Church, and an old Bishop friend of mine used to say 'once a deacon, always a deacon' regardless of how far up the ladder they rose. In fact, these days, some feel called to that path and we have rediscovered the permanent diaconate. The reality in my time, however, and for most now, was that the diaconate was a kind of probationary year before returning to be ordained priest.

A deacon cannot pronounce absolution or celebrate the Eucharist – apart from that the average congregation made no distinction. You wore a cassock with your collar the wrong way round and you'd been ordained. You'd been to theological college and you were supposed to have all the answers. I was made deacon in Wakefield

Cathedral by Bishop Eric Treacy at Michaelmas, 29th September 1971.

We were summoned to St Peter's Convent, Horbury, on the Thursday before the big event, for the Ordination Retreat. As night fell, the Bishop came and gave his Official Charge, detailing all he expected of his clergy, and warning us it would not be easy. We spent Friday in deep prayer and contemplation, wondering mainly what on earth we had let ourselves in for and how far could we get before being discovered if we ran away.

On Saturday afternoon there was some light relief as we re-entered the real world by being ferried into Wakefield Cathedral for a rehearsal of the following day's events. Any visitors to the Cathedral at that time could have been forgiven for thinking they'd walked into a fashion parade, for they would have seen folks prancing around for the first time in their black cassocks and clerical collars – not quite 'Does my bum look big in this?', but almost.

Then it was over to a hotel opposite called Caesar's Palace, which is not there now, for High Tea on the Bishop, before returning to the convent for the last night there. I often reflect on the humour of Bishop Treacy that he invited his ordinands to experience the temptations of Caesar's Palace before being called to holier things.

I don't think any of us slept very well that night, and

then, the day of the ordination – disaster!

There was no hot water! The old monastic boiler was just not up to the strain of providing the needs of the sisters and their guests. Now a cold bath may be thought ideal for purging the sins of the world, the flesh and the devil, but for those of us relying on shaving by razor it meant we didn't quite cut the image by being ordained with bits of sticking-plaster on our faces.

The service of Litany, Eucharist and Ordination started at 10.30am and lasted until about 1pm, and it all passed in a bit of a haze. My parents and Madeleine were in the congregation, and after the official photographs outside and sherry and nibbles with the Bishop, we left – my parents to return to Copley with the vicar who'd kindly brought them in his car; Madeleine to Wakefield Westgate station for her train back to London where she had a bed-sit as she was then working at the Geological Museum in South Kensington; and me to go to Golcar, where I was introduced again to my new parish for the next few years, my new boss, the princely sum of £775 stipend per year and my car!

Chapter 15

Life as a Curate

A house had been provided for me on the 1960s council estate in the parish – at 9 Cedar Close, to be exact. This was the very first reaching out by the church onto that estate, and I think the hope was that I'd somehow convert the residents and lead them into the fold, but, surprise, surprise, this just didn't happen. There were many more of them than of me.

I did manage to set up a House Group/Bible Study, but there was no crossover between them and the main church congregation, with the exception of my vicar, who came down and join us. He was actually very supportive and a kind pastor, and an extremely holy man, but unfortunately he hadn't been blessed with the 'human touch' – he enjoyed very little practical sense.

His housekeeper, a Miss Connie Dent, experienced this first hand. I heard that she once complained she needed a new stepladder, so my vicar went into Huddersfield on the bus and purchased such ladder.

All well and good, but he never thought to have it delivered. Instead he walked back to the Bus Station and tried to board the bus to Golcar during the rush-hour – bearing the ladder. You can imagine the reaction of the conductor. The bus was full, there was no room under the stairs for such a tall item, and it would be unsafe for him to stand on the rear open platform holding it …

Eventually, keen to get the bus away, the conductor allowed him and it on, hoping that no inspector would board during the three mile journey. Fortunately, most of the passengers knew of him, if not him personally, liked him and made allowances.

He didn't stop there though. I've mentioned that Golcar is a very hilly place, stretching from the valley bottom to the moors above. On one occasion, an elderly lady, who just happened to live at the bottom of the parish, expressed a wish to attend the midweek service in the church, which was halfway up the hillside. Now after my arrival, the answer was simple – send me down with the car to collect and return her. But before then, my vicar had a novel solution.

Instead of asking someone else to ferry her, or even ordering a taxi, he walked down carrying a dining chair, and they then set of together to conquer the climb to the church – she walking slowly with her stick and he carrying the chair. Every hundred yards or so, he put the chair down on the pavement and she sat on it, recovering her strength for the next section. And so they eventually arrived at the church with him exhausted and in no condition to conduct a service. Going home was of course, easier, with gravity playing its part. Now you can't help but admire a man who was prepared to go to such extremes to enable a parishioner to receive the sacrament.

The car was a Godsend, and people in the outlying hospitals found themselves visited by their Vicar and Curate/ Chauffeur more regularly than ever before. (A curate, by the way, is a member of the clergy who acts as an assistant to the vicar, so I was an ordained deacon in my first curacy.)

My vicar and I used to meet every day for Matins at 8.30am and Evensong at 5pm in the parish church, as clergy were bound by canon law to recite the offices every day, regardless of whether anyone was present. But if we happened to find ourselves in the car at 5pm, returning from a visit, then the office was still said. He, in the passenger seat would read the Psalms and the 2 lessons, but I was expected to take my part in the alternate verses of the canticles and responses and say 'Amen' to the prayers, all the while steering the car safely through the rush-hour traffic and not taking my hands off the steering wheel.

Now, I've never even managed to drive and hold a serious conversation at the same time, and he never appreciated just how stressful I found it, trying to observe the traffic lights, watch out for stray pedestrians, and remember the next verse of the Magnificat simultaneously!

Having got a 'second in command' at long last, my boss booked a fortnight's holiday for a month after my arrival. He promised to give me detailed instruction on taking a funeral when he returned, but, of course, the inevitable happened and a funeral director rang the day after his departure, and no, they wouldn't wait two weeks, and yes, I'd have to do it. Although I'd been a bystander at a funeral my boss had taken just after I arrived, it was not the same as doing it myself.

I was very anxious about flying solo, for I'd heard the story of a friend from college, then serving in Northumberland, who had fallen into the grave the first burial he took. He was standing too close, didn't realise the artificial turf the gravedigger had placed over the edge was also covering some very wet clayey soil, and his quick thinking response 'just examining the grave beforehand' impressed neither the undertaker nor mourners peering down in amazement from six feet above. So it was some relief that my first was to be a cremation.

Funerals in those days were very long affairs. It started with prayers at the Funeral Home (all the 'best' undertakers had one of these, fully furnished, for their own exclusive use). I drove there, parked up and changed into my canonicals – cassock, surplice and black scarf. I walked through a cigarette smoke curtain at the door, caused by those who couldn't face the following hour or so without a last desperate puff, and entered a large room, full of mourners in their Sunday best – either pulling desperately at their skirts as they realised that what was suitable for a disco was not quite so for a funeral, or dressed uncomfortably in their dark suits reeking of mothballs and tugging at the collars of their white shirts which seemed to have shrunk since the last funeral several years ago.

Pride of place in the centre of the room would be the open coffin. I was then expected to come up with a few carefully chosen words of wisdom and comfort, to which I added the odd prayer or two, after which the Funeral Director entered with the solemn words, 'Does anyone else wish to view him before we screws him down?'

Then I led the coffin and mourners into the hearse, and sat between the Funeral Director and driver for the journey to the church, gravely leading them up the church path (note I didn't say 'garden path'), avoiding dragging my cassock hems through all the puddles, into the church before conducting the full funeral service there.

Then I had to repeat the performance of back into the hearse for the ride to the crematorium – in Huddersfield, this was at Fixby, the other side of the town from Golcar. The slow journey through Friday afternoon traffic could take up to 30 minutes, especially if there were roadworks, with the FD not exactly easing the tension on the way, by becoming more and more anxious by the minute that they'd lose their slot.

Then I led the way again into the crematorium for the committal service. I learned that you had just a few moments to comb your hair and compose yourself while the FD was making sure all the followers had made it (the experienced ones counted the cars leaving the church, and if the same number arrived at the crematorium then there was no need for the search party). He was also organising the order of procession.

Everything went well enough – the coffin was where it should be on the catafalque and I was ready. It turned out though that crematorium attendants were just as cunning when greeting new clergy as an engineer might be when initiating new apprentices in the factory. But instead of being sent to the stores for a left-handed screwdriver, or a long weight, I was told by a solemn faced attendant that the motor which was supposed to power the conveyor belt carrying the coffin from catafalque through the door to the cremators on the other side of the wall had failed, and I would have to wind it in by hand.

'Ok,' I thought. 'I can do that.'

But he had another trick up his sleeve. He pointed to the handle he'd previously stuck to the skirting board on the other side of the chapel from the catafalque. Fortunately, out of my eye-corner, just as I was wondering how, with any dignity, I could bend double, my back to the congregation, and say the words of committal whilst winding the handle, I spotted him grinning from ear to ear.

(I did get my revenge on my second visit, when I rushed in and greeted him by asking whether he'd been told that they'd recently changed their minds from having a said committal and now wanted to sing two hymns, leaving him frantically scuttling round for the appropriate CDs. Oh, how we laughed.)

On this particular day, after the final service, it was back into the empty hearse, where, between the Funeral Director and driver, I heard some of the bluest jokes imaginable. I realise now that it was their way of coping with the tension, especially if it had been a particularly harrowing occasion, but I also suspect the local undertakers had a wager on who could shock the clergy the most.

The fourth venue of the afternoon was the Princess Café in Huddersfield, for refreshments, for according to Yorkshire legend you hadn't done him proud unless you'd 'buried him with ham' and a glass or two of sherry. So you returned home at about 6pm, rather the worse for wear and not wanting anything else to eat that day, some four hours after you'd left, having taken just one funeral. Time-Motion experts would question the efficient use of professional time, but it was an excellent way of getting to know far more people than you would by sitting in church in a month of Sundays.

Having graduated from the rubber doll,
I'm now let loose on Golcar's finest

Chapter 16

Communion

In those days there was a saying that there was only one thing worse than being a curate, and that was having one – something I was able to test later in my ministry. The first year at Golcar was certainly a steep learning curve for me, but my boss, the Revd John Mowll, was a kind and patient teacher – an ideal man to guide you through the first steps.

He was, however, a stickler for detail. His faith lay in an all-knowing God who had created the universe in all its intricate detail and splendour, and deserved to be worshipped by paying attention to meticulous detail. For example, there was a special way to fold the corporal – the linen cloth kept inside the burse which was unfolded on to the altar before the chalice and paten were laid upon them. Likewise the missal stand which held the altar book, or missal, was ceremoniously moved from the west side of the altar to the east between the reading of the epistle and gospel, ready for the gospel to be read from the east, the source of sunlight and the Light of the World.

I remember one morning after I'd been priested, when I'd overslept and arrived at church with just enough time to change into cassock, alb and stole, he refused to allow me to take the communion service because I had not shaved.

'Shave – Celebrate,' he said, referring to the fact you did not take a communion service, or lead one, but rather celebrated it.

In fact, the whole of liturgy was a holy work for God. I often wonder what he would have thought of my later years, when I experimented with the growing of a beard!

Those conducting worship were supposed to be ready, and in the chancel engaged in private prayer, asking that you may be a worthy channel of the grace of God about to flow through you. I often think of him in churches where they have the same motto now, 'Speak to God before the service and speak to one another afterwards'. For how can the mere layfolk learn to wait upon God in silent prayer before the service when the priest or vicar is flapping about placing their markers in the lectern bible or holding a last minute confab with the organist regarding the number of verses to be sung?

This, of course, is more difficult in parishes where

the priest exercises a 'hit-and-run' ministry, arriving hot and sweaty from parish 'A' with five minutes to spare before the start of the service in parish 'B', knowing that if the sermon were longer than four minutes, he or she would be late arriving at parish 'C' for the third service that morning. Tough luck if anyone wants to talk an important matter through with you between the services.

Another rule of John Mowll was ensure your shoes are polished before celebrating the communion. The reason? Well, people were unlikely to go away impressed if their abiding memory of the service was neither the splendour of the music nor the power of the preaching but the scruffiness of the vicar's shoes as they knelt to receive communion, eyes cast downwards as the dispensing priest passed closely by on the other side of the altar rail.

Later on, I sometimes took to wearing sandals on my bare feet during warm weather – I also thought they gave a monastic atmosphere – but was not overly thrilled to discover later that my congregation had gone away, commenting on being able to see my toes as they received the sacred Body and Blood of our Lord.

The first major ceremony after my arrival at Golcar was the harvest festival. The church was crowded for all services, and people willingly brought boxes of fruit, flowers, etc, to the altar rail. Which was lovely, but did pose a problem the week afterwards as to what to do with them. Some parishes now auction off all the produce at the Harvest Supper and give the proceeds to charity, or, more likely, church funds. (So you dedicate the fruit of your orchards to God on the Sunday, and then buy it back again on the Monday night, which I suppose is strangely in keeping with the Old Testament law concerning the firstborn – where the firstborn animal of your flock or the first-fruits of your crop belonged to God and must be sacrificed, and if you had neither, you gave money.)

Other parishes gave the produce to residential homes, or dumped it on them, to be honest, and whereas potatoes and vegetables were usually welcome, there was a limit to the number of bunches of grapes they could receive. The concept of foodbanks was unknown then, so we ended up loading all the produce in the boot of the car on a Monday morning, and spent the whole week resembling a mobile greengrocer's van as we drove round the homes of all the elderly people, handing out apples here and a bunch of grapes there, and so on.

Our system did little to solve the problem of all the pumpkins the folks loved to bring, as there was a limit to the number of pumpkins you could unload on to the elderly before they started to hurl them back at you. And if they did accept one, what would they do with it? This reminds me that I later heard an excellent recipe for pumpkins from a harvest produce auctioneer – you carefully wash it, dry it, cut it, scrape out all the flesh and then throw it in the bin!

So was our harvest distribution a good use of our time and abilities? Probably not, but we liked to think that it was the thought which counted.

Interspersed between learning as I went along within the parish, I was also expected to attend a number of courses the diocese laid on in the first year. This was officially known as 'Post-Ordination Training', or 'Potty Training' as it was affectionately known, and there were also various retreats at places such as The Community of the Resurrection at Mirfield, or Whirlow Grange, the retreat-house for the Sheffield diocese.

One such meeting with the Bishop and diocesan staff I well remember was when we had raised the question of a book allowance – after all, we were supposed to keep up to date in our studies.

To our surprise, Bishop Eric Treacy was very keen on this, and fully supported us, much to the consternation of the Chair of the Diocesan Board of Finance, who was wondering where the extra cash would be found – until the Archdeacon had a word in Bishop Eric's ear and explained we had asked for a book allowance, and not, as he had misheard, a boot allowance.

For Eric Treacy was a bishop who placed much emphasis on visiting the common man, rather than sitting in the rectory study. This showed in his public ministry. I remember how he spent every Christmas morning, not preaching in the cathedral or important parish churches, but visiting Wakefield prison, seeking out the lonely at that particularly difficult time.

As there were only 4 of us to be priested, the retreat was held in Bishop's Lodge. I think Bishop Eric would have liked it to be more austere, but his wife May spoiled us to the hilt, ensuring we had warm comfortable rooms and as much food as we wanted.

We dined at their table, with May, whose love and devotion for and to her husband was obvious to all, regaling us with stories about what happened when 'we' inducted Mr so and so at such a parish, or 'we' confirmed ten people at x last Sunday, the Bishop simply gazing across at her, with a query on his face which said 'hang on. I thought I'd done that', but saying nothing.

So I returned to Golcar after my priesting, now authorised to play a full part in the conducting of worship, but with still much to learn. I might be a priest, but 'once a deacon, always a deacon'

Chapter 17

Married Life

By this time, Madeleine and I were planning our marriage. She was working with the British Geological Survey based at the Geological Museum in South Kensington, and managed to arrange a transfer to their smaller West Yorkshire branch at Cross Gates. This was just outside Leeds, and she was prepared to commute the twenty or so miles from Golcar every day.

The date was fixed – Golcar parish church, 10am on the Feast of St Swithun, 15th July 1974. It was just a small celebration, with our families and a few friends, plus my boss, who conducted the ceremony, and his housekeeper.

We later repaired to a hotel on the outskirts of Huddersfield for a splendid lunch. It was a typical Yorkshire summer's day – thunder and lightning and pouring rain during the morning, and steady rain for the rest of the day.

Swithun was a 9th century Anglo-Saxon bishop of

Winchester who later became the patron of its cathedral. According to legend, he was a humble man, much loved by his people, who, on his deathbed gave orders that his grave should be along the north wall of his cathedral, where the poor would pass by and the raindrops from the eaves fall upon it.

However, about 100 years later, the good folk of Winchester decided a pauper's grave was inappropriate for someone who had become something of a legend, with several miracles ascribed to him, and moved his remains to a new shrine within. And, again, according to legend, his translation was made difficult by a tremendous downpour, which did not abate for some time – a sign that the saint was displeased with what they were doing. Hence the popular weather-lore:

St Swithun's day if thou dost rain
For forty days it will remain
St Swithun's day if thou be fair
For forty days 'twill rain nae mare

They were even more explicit in Buckinghamshire:

If on St Swithun's day it really pours
You're better off to stay indoors.

Well, we didn't stay indoors. We went on honeymoon. To the Isle of Skye. Part of the magic of the journey in those days used to be crossing the narrow strait between Kyle of Lochalsh and Kyleakin not by rowing boat – I'm not that old! – but by a small ship. You queued up on the slipway and waited to drive on to the small Caledonian Macbrayne's ferry for the 15 minute journey. During the busy times you waited for quite a while as the ferry could only convey twenty or so cars at one time, and the local conditions meant that nothing bigger or heavier could be used. Nowadays, of course, you just drive yourself over on the bridge.

Our destination was Elgol, on the South-West shore, and we were booked to stay with a Mrs McArthur, who kept a small B&B. Every morning, after a substantial breakfast, we would set out to walk in the delightful scenery of the Cuillins. Every day we'd get soaked to the skin, as there's nothing much else to do in the Cuillins when it rains, and every teatime we'd end up back on Mrs McArthur's doorstep.

She in turn would open the door and sing the praises of the good Saint Swithun, 'Och, yer waiaiait!' as she raised her arms ready to lower the creel to dry out our coats and boots ready for a repeat performance the following day.

Despite the rather soggy start, we had a very happy

marriage, ended only by Madeleine's premature death 22 years later.

Chapter 18

Back to Golcar

There were quite a few fascinating characters within and without the church in Golcar. One such was Doreen Swallow. A 'straight-up' Yorkshire woman who spoke her mind to both mill owner and bishop, and, having no difficulty in distinguishing between a spade and a b— shovel, she was employed as sacristan and cleaner.

She was extremely conscientious and meticulous in her work, but neither suffered fools nor took prisoners. The vicar and I liked to think we were in charge of the church, and she graciously allowed us to continue in that delusion, but it was Doreen who really ruled. Anyone would have been forgiven for thinking that the Last Judgement could hold no greater terrors after being on the receiving end of one of her tongue-lashings if they came in from the muddy churchyard and walked over her freshly washed floors with their dirty shoes.

We even took to keeping a pair of carpet slippers

by the vestry door. We'd often have a small chuckle at Evensong on the 16th evening of the month when we recited:

Yea, the sparrow hath found her an house, and the
swallow a nest where she may lay her young;
Even thy altars, O Lord of hosts, my King and my God

Psalm 84 v 3

A good musician/organist is essential in the offering of worship, for we worship the Almighty not only with our voices but with our abilities too.

In my time, Golcar was blessed with several good organists, which meant they could work out a rota amongst themselves, and no one felt 'put-upon' for a month of Sundays or so. For most of our organists, leading worship on a Sunday meant rehearsing for a few hours or so in the week before, but for one, a Kenneth Sykes, it meant a few day's rehearsal. This was not because he was a poor organist – indeed he was exceptionally good. Rather it was because he was totally blind. He would turn up for Evensong, and the stairs to the organ loft, led by his faithful guide dog, who would then quietly lie by the pedalboard whilst his master played, and no doubt bored to tears with my sermons, (the dog, I mean, not

Kenneth, I hope), and then lead him back home when the duty was ended.

For Kenneth, who was a music teacher by profession, his rehearsal for the coming Sunday started the previous Monday. He had a Braille copy of the hymnbook, words and music, and knew most of the hymn tunes and words off by heart. In fact he could play them better than me, and I was trying to read the music. Canticles and responses were no challenge either, as these varied little Sunday by Sunday. The greatest challenge was the playing of the psalm to Anglican chant. This differed each Sunday (as there are 150 of them), and a sighted person needed a pair of eyes to sight-read the chant, another pair of eyes to read the words and put the words to the music, (all the while paying due regard to the pointing – where to change chord, where to pause for effect, where to allow the choir to take a breath, etc), and a third pair of eyes to keep a watch on the keyboard, change the stops, etc.

You also needed to play the bass notes on the pedalboard, but this was done by feel and the feet, so no eyes needed.

All of this left Kenneth with a major challenge. So he firstly had to learn the words of the psalm by heart, with all the 'thees' and 'thous' etc. Then he had to learn the chords of the chant. Then he had to learn how to put the two together with the pointing. All in all, a particularly onerous task, and I took my hat off to him (well, gentlemen are supposed to remove their hats in church), as I could not recall his making a single mistake.

I actually felt a bit self-conscious talking with Kenneth at first, and was very careful to watch my vocabulary, trying to be sympathetic to his disability and not wishing to cause any hurt or embarrassment, but when he'd broken the ice by making a few comments like 'I see the miners are out on strike' or 'I notice the weather forecast says it's going to rain', I realised he did not let it get in his way, and we conversed normally.

We became good friends. Some Friday lunchtimes, I would collect fish and chips from the local chippy, and take them to his house as he returned from teaching, and we'd dine together, talking music and my listening to his adventurous tales. He did not allow his impediment to stop him getting around – his teaching meant he had to make frequent trips into Huddersfield, and he used to regale me with accounts of what had happened to him.

Huddersfield was a particular taxing place in the early 1970s, as a lot of buildings were being pulled down and new ones erected. Not only did all the bus-stops change, but the entire bus station moved at one stage. His dog did her best, guiding him the best she could, but it was very demanding on the poor animal when she tried to lead him safely down a street which was there only a fortnight before, but was now a building site. Apparently one morning, after much frustration of this kind, she just gave up, sat on the pavement and told Kenneth 'Sorry mate, but you're on your own' Fortunately a kind passer-by guided her and Kenneth to the music shop he desired to reach.

It was also interesting when they eventually managed to find the bus-stop for home and joined the queue. For Huddersfield Corporation Transport, as they were in pre 1974, was experimenting with one-person controlled double deckers, with boarding through the front door, where you paid your dues to the driver. To speed things up you were supposed to alight through a centre door, halfway down the nearside of the lower saloon. This allowed boarding and leaving to be simultaneous. All well and good, but no one had told the dog.

On one occasion, when Kenneth and dog were about 5th in the queue, a bus pulled up, both sets of doors opened, and the dog saw the opening in the side of the bus and as no one was alighting, took her opportunity thinking she'd be praised for being a canny canine, and whisked Kenneth into the bus that way. She was a strong dog and there was nothing Kenneth could do but follow, accompanied by much grumbling from the people ahead of him and cries of 'queue-jumper' and 'fare evader'.

Fortunately, the driver was alert and had spotted what was happening in his interior mirror, so did not trap dog or Kenneth in the closing centre doors.

A highlight of my friendship with Kenneth was taking him to Leeds Town Hall one Friday evening. He'd expressed a desire to hear the famous clarinettist Jack Brymer play Copland's Clarinet Concerto, so we booked tickets and I took him in the car, and it was a very enjoyable evening.

The small town/ large village of Golcar was only called such by those from outside. To the locals it was always 'Goka'. Its name is thought to have originally derived from St Guthlac, who visited the area in the 8th century. By the time of the Domesday Book, it had become known as 'Goullakarres' (quite a name to get your tongue round to the conductor on the bus), then later 'Guldescar' then 'Golcar' to 'Goka'.

Now Guthlac was a Christian hermit from Crowland Abbey near Market Deeping, and was particularly venerated in the fenlands of Eastern England. What caused him to visit West Yorkshire I do not know, but legend tells he did visit the area around the year 700AD, and preached to the people of the Colne Valley from a promontory, or scar, on the hillside. Hence 'Guthlac's Scar' becoming Golcar etc …

There's a road junction near the spot now, joining Scar Lane with Knowl Road and James Street. There is also a pub, imaginatively called 'The Junction Inn' and a fish and chip shop opposite (not the one from which I bought Kenneth's lunch – another one – In my Father's house there were many chip shops).

Now because I was younger than my boss, and had just emerged from college, and therefore knew all about communicating with children, it was my joy to go into school every Thursday morning to take the assembly, thus relieving the teachers of a legal task they looked forward to with little glee. The assembly was prepared well in advance (oh, yes?) and I went in full of joy and enthusiasm (in theory).

In practice, I was usually up half the night before wondering how I could educate them and keep their attention for the 20 minutes or so this week. But then I was young. I was fresh out of training. I was recently ordained. I knew all the answers. So one day I thought I'd regale them with the legend of Guthlac, teaching them a little bit of local history, a little bit of geography and a little bit of Christianity thrown-in for good measure. What could possibly go wrong?

Halfway through my assembly I noticed their eyes glazing over (I'd done well to keep their attention that far), so to try to reconnect, I told them all this may have happened somewhere near where the fish and chip shop is situated today, wrapped it all up with a quick prayer and a blessing, and made my exit.

The following week, the headteacher called me into the school to examine their exercise books. Every single child had written 'At about 7pm, Guthlac came from afar and preached outside the chip shop'. The image of Harold the fryer turning to his wife and saying 'Eh-up – better put some more chips on – it's going to be a good night' stayed with me for some time afterwards.

Actually, at this stage, with having had no children with Madeleine, I had no idea about communicating with young people, and had received next to no training at college. Little did I know then that at a later stage, I would be welcomed by Tim and Lorna, who became my very wonderful and accommodating stepchildren, and even later by two grandchildren, who have tried to drag me into the 21st century, via a very steep learning curve indeed!

One final story, which happened, not in Golcar, but in a similar village, concerned a local mill owner, who, in an act of gratitude to the Almighty, endowed the local church with a splendid new green altar-frontal. Now it is customary to embroider the letters 'IHS' on such things, usually in a prominent place in the centre. These letters form a monogram for the Name of Jesus, from the first three letters of the name in Greek – iota, eta, sigma. The 'I' is aspirated, and sometimes reproduced in a way that it could be mistaken for a capital 'J' and the eta is written as what appears to be a capital 'H' in English, and the whole name pronounced something like 'HI-e'er-sou' (many apologies to cringing Greek scholars) – hence 'IHS'.

Now, as Michael Caine may say 'not a lot of people know that', hence the story that after this splendid gift had been dedicated and placed in full view of the admiring congregation at the front of the altar, there was one poor lady who was deeply offended, and complained to the vicar of the blatant advertising by the local mill owner in a very inappropriate place.

Puzzled by these accusations, the cleric followed the lady into church, where she pointed an accusing finger at the offending gold embroidered monogram, saying 'There! Joshua Hoyle and Sons' (the name of the local woollen mill).

Looking forward to a long and happy retirement

Chapter 19

Moving on

My time at Golcar saw the industrial upheavals of the early 1970s, under the premiership of Edward Heath, when high rates of inflation and capped pay increases mean that for many, the gap between income and cost of living increased. One group of workers particularly badly affected amongst many were the miners. As I remember, they didn't strike as such (as in a decade later in 1984), but operated a strict work to rule policy, which meant production was reduced. Consequently the supply of coal to the power stations was limited.

To conserve electricity, industries had to resort to working a three day week, and domestic supplies were rationed. Each area was allowed power for a four hour period before it would be cut for the next four hours – details were published in the local newspapers. Consequently this caused much disruption to social activities, but it was not all bad news as firewood suppliers, candle makers and sellers of torches and batteries did a great trade. And it also meant some church council meetings had to be cancelled.

But, on the whole this social disruption caused feelings to run very high against the miners, with the usual remarks along the lines of 'holding the country to ransom' etc, etc.

It was during this upheaval that I was invited to go down a mine by a mine safety engineer, who happened to be a member of our congregation, to see at first hand just what conditions were like in the industry. So with a certain amount of trepidation, but feeling I could not refuse such an invitation, I turned up at the pithead of a certain South Yorkshire colliery, to exchange any matches, watches and other valuables for a hard hat with attached light, gloves and rubber knee protectors. Handy, I thought, should the need arise for a quick prayer whilst I was down there – little did I know how useful they would really be.

Although I was beginning to doubt my sanity at this stage, the real enormity of what I was doing struck home when I was then asked to sign a disclaimer form, indemnifying the colliery and its employees of any liability should there be any accident or mishap whilst I was on their premises. I'd never had to do this when visiting parishioners in hospital, or entering another church to preach! And, thinking about it, if the worst had happened, my own personal life insurance would not have paid out either.

So down we went in the cage and gathering gloom for what seemed miles into the earth. When the contraption finally stopped, we found a dimly lit passageway, along which we walked for about a mile or so. It was not a pleasant walk, but not too bad, I thought. Then my companion warned 'mind your head' as the roof became lower and lower until I was eventually walking bent double. The air was becoming musty, and I started wishing I could see a glimmer of light at the end of the tunnel. Then we stopped.

Good, I thought, we can go back again now. But no, for my companion pointed to a hole about 2 feet in diameter rather like a large mouse hole in the skirting board.

'In you go,' he said, in such a matter-of-fact way, so it was down on all fours, crawling along this narrow passageway with only the light on my helmet for company, with the real reason for the knee protectors becoming obvious.

I hoped my companion was behind me, but I had no way of knowing, and it was not a good time to realise you suffered from claustrophobia. Slowly my eyes began to get accustomed to the total darkness, and then as I slowly crept along, I began to be aware of lights in the walls above and alongside me, rather like a fairy grotto. But the faces they revealed were not of elves. Rather they were streaked with sweat and coal dust, and belonging to bare-chested miners as they were laboriously digging with picks and hammers at the walls surrounding them. And I'm sure one or two of them grinned at what must have been a look of horror on my face.

It took me about 20 minutes to creep through that tunnel, but it seemed like a lifetime. They were down there at that coal-face for 8 hours at a time, for what would really be, for them, a lifetime.

I emerged fully disoriented, not knowing if it was teatime or Maundy Thursday, just grateful to see daylight again. And as I enjoyed the luxury of a pithead shower, I realised the miners were worth every penny they earned. Interestingly, I heard later that those on that shift had heard a priest was about to visit them, and knowing the rumour that the seam was to be shortly closed, assumed I'd gone to minister the Last Rites to it.

In those days it was customary for a curate to serve two 3-year curacies, gaining experience of a second parish after the first. However, due to the increasing age of my boss, and his obvious need of help during those years,

I agreed (with the Bishop's permission) to spend longer with him. I served almost all my six years in Golcar.

My boss himself announced his retirement shortly after I left, so the parish had a complete change of care. Matters were brought to a head for me when Madeleine heard the branch of the Geological Survey at Cross Gates where she had been working was to close, and move to what was the Mary Ward Teacher Training College at Keyworth, in South Nottinghamshire.

There was no option for her but to go, as it seemed wrong to expect her to give up her career (and it was too far to expect her to commute!). I, on the other hand, was in the position of being able to choose where I worked to a certain extent, and so I approached the Bishop of Leicester about the possibility of employment in his diocese.

There may be some reading this and tutting, thinking – 'The Lord should be calling him as to where he works', but I happen to believe God's plan is seen in everyday events, and that the Good Lord helps those who are prepared to do some of the spadework themselves.

Hence, the Rt Revd Richard Rutt invited me to look at the parish of Hathern, just on the Leicestershire-Nottinghamshire border, about three miles north of Loughborough, and within easy commuting distance for Madeleine to Keyworth.

Chapter 20

A New Home

Hathern at that time was a village of about 2000 people with two or three green fields between it and Loughborough. The post was as Priest-in-Charge, as it was expected there would be some pastoral re-organisation afoot. The economic climate meant the days of one paid person per parish were quickly becoming history, especially in rural areas, and paid clergy were being expected to look after groups of parishes, with the help of unpaid lay-people working in teams.

So a Priest-in-Charge did the same ministry as a Rector or Vicar, for the same stipend, but his terms of employment were different as he did not have the freehold of the living. When I was appointed, I was told that Hathern might be linked with Loughborough, working half my time in Hathern and the rest of the time in Loughborough. Or alternatively Hathern might be joined with two other parishes, Long Whatton and Diseworth to the north-west in the direction of the East

Midlands Airport.

A link with Loughborough didn't seem a good idea at the time as Hathern people were still jealously guarding those two or three green fields and fiercely valued their independence, so when the time came for the Vicar of Long Whatton and Diseworth to retire some three years later, I counselled a link-up with them.

Hence, I then became Rector of Hathern, Long Whatton and Diseworth.

Apart from all three villages wanting a Main communion service at the same time on a Sunday (ie. at about 10.30am), they soon saw that compromise was the way forward, and I got to work happily building up a ministry team including six lay readers and other helpers, along with the support of co-operative churchwardens.

The team grew further a little later, when I was joined by a non-stipendiary priest – someone who was in paid employment elsewhere but felt called to the church, and contributed what they could in the time they had. Later still, two other parishes Belton and Osgathorpe joined the group, along with a woman deacon who was ordained priest when the legislation allowed in the 1990s.

The Rectory at Hathern was then a large, rambling house, built, I think, in the 1830s at a time when the Rector had private income and was able to afford to employ gardeners, cooks, cleaners, housekeepers etc to look after the place. Indeed, one of my predecessors had used the premises as a kind of preparatory school to ensure students from abroad had a sufficient command of English to enter the local universities. Whilst I am unsure of the success of his efforts, lack of accommodation could not be regarded as one of the shortcomings of his venture.

Half of this enormous house had been sealed off when central heating (of sorts) was installed in the 1960s, but even then Madeleine and I were left with a very large study, sitting room, dining room, kitchen and utility room downstairs and five bedrooms of varying sizes upstairs, along with toilet and bathroom. The whole place could have been made very comfortable but for one thing lacking – the thousands of pounds which we did not have, and which the diocesan property board may have had but were not prepared to spend. For to them, the house was a 'problem' house, at the top of their list for early replacement. To me, in my younger days, it was a place where I ran from room to room, wearing as many jumpers as possible. Only Madeleine saw its real potential and had a vision for the place – to her it was the North West Leicestershire Animal Refuge.

To say she was fond of animals is an understatement. No cat which ventured up the drive at any time of day or night was refused a good meal and warm bed, whether it was a stray or not. And if it wished to stay it was accepted with no questions asked. We already had a rough collie when we arrived, which also had been rescued and which was frightened of the cats. Honestly, the memory of a fully grown dog cowering in the corner of a room while three or four well-fed tabbies patrolled around him – there was no question that they owned the place!

Various injured birds from the garden spent a time of convalescence with us. We had hens occupying a dilapidated henhouse at the top of the garden. We had inherited these from the previous vicar, and every so often Madeleine would come home from work via the livestock market at Melton Mowbray with a further four or so she had bought. No hen was put down – they all died of old age, for when they had finished laying, they were transferred to a superannuated status where they spent the rest of their natural life in the gardens. I wondered if we would have to ask a local joiner to make them little wooden zimmer-frames.

We were both vegetarian – something which seemed to have escaped the local squire, for every Christmas there'd be a brace of pheasant for the Rector's table. We'd come home on a cold, dark December day, put the key in the lock and feel blindly for the door handle, finding instead two pheasant hanging by their necks from it. We always wrote the customary letter of thanks – we didn't have the heart to tell him, as he meant well and once we'd accepted them the first year we couldn't really write the second year saying 'by the way, we're veggies'.

So we didn't know what to do with them. Asking him for a book token instead was out of the question. We couldn't take them back after Christmas and exchange them for something else, like a bottle of wine. We tried giving them to poor families in the parish, who just stared at them, thought of all the plucking and cleaning involved, and said 'No, thanks'.

I tried acting the part and giving them to the local mechanic who serviced my car, but he uttered a few choice expletives and returned them in no uncertain terms (in fact, he made it clear he preferred remuneration of the more traditional kind that could be folded and placed in his pocket).

In the end, we simply left them on the lawn overnight and let the local foxes feast on them. There seemed a sort of poetic justice there – his Lordship's birds feeding the animals he'd hunted off his land.

There was a large vegetable garden to the side of the house, but, search as hard as I did in all the outhouses, I could not find the accompanying gardener. We did what we could, but nature won the day as she usually does. I was comforted when Bishop Richard paid a pastoral visit and we sat in the study, drinking coffee and gazing out at what could have been a wonderful display of vegetables, but which was largely overgrown, and felt I should apologise for its state.

'Don't,' he said, 'otherwise I'd be getting worried you were neglecting your parish duties.'

I liked Richard, and was sorry when he later left the C of E.

We also had a large lawn, in the centre of which was a magnificent cedar tree. The parishioners were fond of the lawn and seemed to be particularly keen we should maintain it, especially in the month or so before the annual church garden fete was due. So they actually bought me a petrol mower – not one I could sit on, that would be spoiling me – but one I could push.

It took about a day a fortnight in the growing season to keep on top of that lawn, and when, after a few such days, I conducted an appraisal and concluded it was actually a bad use of my time, time which could have been spent writing better sermons or visiting the sick, and nothing to do with my simply being a lazy b— as some folk cruelly proclaimed, we decided to invest in two self-propelling lawnmowers – sheep.

Two sheep would not be out of place in our zoo, after

all. We knew a couple in the parish who were members of the Rare Breeds Association, and they found for us a Herdwick and a Southdown. We called the larger of the two 'Tommy' after Bishop Richard's successor, and the smaller 'Godfrey' after his assistant. It seemed rather appropriate naming our two sheep after the diocesan and assistant Shepherd of Souls.

We bought what was described on the box as an 'Electric Shepherd' – I suppose these days it would be an e-shepherd – which actually consisted of a few hundred feet of wire, some plastic posts and a battery capable of supplying a little reminder to any errant sheep that they should not be considering going beyond its bounds. This was a necessary precaution actually, since, for some reason, people had the habit of visiting me during the daytime, leaving the gate open, and we'd then find the sheep taking on extra parochial duties, whether desired or not.

At night, with the gate firmly closed, we let them wander around the grounds, on a kind of pick-and-mix basis. When the growing season was over, we had to supplement their diet of course, with a bucket of special mixture every morning with something like ovine muesli, which they seemed to enjoy.

We'd had a heat-detection light installed outside the rectory door for security purposes, and when we opened the door in the winter, the light would come on, they'd see it from the far side of the lawn, and come running and bleating to greet us, or, more accurately, breakfast. Now if they thought the service was a bit tardy of a morning, they'd approach the door, unknowingly switch the light on with their body heat and think its luminescence meant we were coming out. When we did not appear, they banged against the door with their hooves. So it was a vicious circle. The light stayed on. They thought we were coming. Their persistent knocking threatened to damage the door. We had no option but to leave our warm bed and feed them.

At least I did not have a problem in rising for the early mass, as some of my brethren had ...

Every spring, we'd hold a shearing and dipping party on the lawn, for we provided the facilities for other members of the Association to bring their charges in exchange for having Tommy and Godfrey included in the proceedings.

From childhood, Madeleine had always wanted a horse, and now we took the disused stable, which my predecessor had converted into a garage, as a sign to exchange fantasy for reality. So our cars were quickly evicted and the building found itself restored to its original purpose to welcome the latest member of the zoo. Henry was a large, sweet grey with two speeds – very slow and stop. Madeleine would go for a ride (or, more accurately a slow saunter), and on one occasion, as she was coming down the lane past a semi-detached house on her way home, the owner saw them passing by, and offered Henry a carrot, thinking he looked hungry. This is a sign of just how slowly they were proceeding, as the owner had time to spot them through his living room window, go into the kitchen to find and clean a carrot, and appear at his front door before Henry had passed the front gate.

Henry was most appreciative of the said offering, and to show his appreciation, insisted on stopping there on every occasion they came down that lane to ensure the donor did not feel rebuffed. That was Henry – what he lacked in velocity he more than made up for in memory. In the meanwhile, Madeleine wisely learned to check if the owner was on holiday before returning via that route, otherwise she would not have got back at all.

I was encouraged to exercise him during the day while she was at work, and considered doing my parish visits on him, but by the time I'd managed to drag him out of the stable, saddle him up and get him moving, the patient I was intending to visit had either recovered or died.

I thought of the Revd Ian Graham-Orlebar who figures in the Revd Fergus Butler-Gallie's compendium of eccentric clerics 'A *Field Guide to the English Clergy*'. Graham-Orelbar was rector of Barton-le-Clay, a rural parish in Bedfordshire, who loved horses and frequently rode through his parish. Apparently, he called his first horse 'Ministry' so that whenever the Archdeacon rang to check up on him, his housekeeper could truthfully say he was out exercising his Ministry. The second he named 'Sabbatical' so that any queries were fielded with 'he's on Sabbatical'. I knew a cleric in Leicester who loved playing golf, so any enquirers at the vicarage were informed he was on a course. I didn't need any of this subterfuge however. One of my churchwardens shared my interest in railways, so that when he could get the time off, I was out with him, on a training day.

Chapter 21

Travelling With the Flock

I've already mentioned our love of North Devon, and after holidaying in Lynmouth for several years, we eventually bought a cottage in Parracombe, just off the A39 from Lynton to Barnstaple. It was called Paradise Cottage, and for a few years lived up to its name. We spent as much time there as possible, but did not want to leave the animals in care, so took them with us.

Henry, of course, went to livery, but the hens went in a well-ventilated box in the boot of the car, the cats were lined up in baskets on the back seat, and the dog lay precariously on top – fortunately he was very good tempered and knew not to make a fuss, otherwise a barbed claw would shoot out from a basket below rather like something from a horror movie.

We occupied the front seats with what luggage we could carry and any convalescing wild birds which happened to be in residence at the time. And the sheep?

Well, Madeleine had a trailer especially constructed that would just accommodate the two of them, and we towed it behind us.

The last to be loaded into the car were always the cats. Sure enough, the sight of the baskets was enough for them to do a vanishing act, and so we spent an exciting game of 'Hunt the Tabby' before eventually setting off. And despite our pleading with them to make themselves comfortable before the journey began, they would inevitably make their protest in the most effective way imaginable, so we rarely got beyond Hathern Turn and one mile out, before having to stop to change the newspaper linings.

The journey was slow – it had to be, as the wheels on the sheep trailer were small and so our speed was limited by law – and, besides, any speed higher than 40mph or so burst the tyres. So it was a long, but surprisingly restful journey down the M42 & M5 motorways (restful from the point of view of not having to change lanes on the motorway – we just stayed in lane 1 and watched everything surge past us).

We usually broke our journey at Michael Wood Services on the M5, where we parked as far away from everyone else as possible, as we stopped to exercise the dog, change the newspapers in the cats' baskets yet again, and beg the sheep to stop banging against the side of the trailer with their hooves. Children in the distant cars would say, 'Mummy, I can hear sheep', and mummy would reply, 'Don't be silly darling', then, 'Yes, you're right', as children dashed over to see this travelling menagerie. If we could only have sold tickets we'd have recouped the cost of the petrol twice over.

After about six hours (on a good journey), we'd arrive at Paradise Cottage and begin the loading process in reverse, although the cats did not need as much encouragement to leave their baskets as they did to enter them. Then it was time to switch on the power, check for any leaking pipes (for, despite turning it off and draining down before leaving, there always seemed to be at least one). Then we'd light a fire, prepare a quick supper and fall into bed.

Despite all this we thoroughly enjoyed our time there, relaxing and walking through the tremendous scenery. We were very aware of taking up a cottage for holiday purposes (although we did spend far more time there than the average second-home owner) so we made a point of using the village store for every purchase to try to help their economy. This pleased the owner no end, for we soon discovered the locals used him just to buy their newspapers and cigarettes, and went into Tesco's in Barnstaple for everything else.

Back in Hathern, one morning after I'd finished a school assembly at the local school, a young mother came up to me and pushed an envelope into my hand. Just as I was wondering if it was a bribe to leave the parish, she said cryptically, 'For your wife'.

When she saw the puzzlement in my face, she added, 'A ticket to the Tupperware party at my house next Thursday.'

I asked her if she'd got the right wife, for 'Tupperware' and 'Madeleine' were words which until then had not been found on the same page together, let alone in the same sentence. But I accepted it with some amazement, and gave it to her that evening. Seeing my obvious confusion, Madeleine smiled and explained that the previous Saturday, while walking the dog past the school, she'd come across a cat she thought was a stray and looked thirsty, and so she had rushed into the school building to get some water for it. But she found no container, so went into the hall, where a sale of various Tupperware pots was being held, and barged to the front of the queue to buy a basin, which she promptly filled and placed in front of the cat. It's probably still there now in the undergrowth. Just don't tell the Tupperware disciples of Hathern, who thought they'd made an enthusiastic convert.

Chapter 22

Big names

Most potted autobiographies have a section where the author has a little name-dropping session. Now this is usually most infuriating – as I was only saying to the Most Revd Justin Welby the other day …

So please indulge me.

Whilst I was at Long Whatton, Lord Crawshaw of Whatton House kindly gave some of his land near the church for the building of affordable homes so the young of the village could stay and not have to move out. When they were finished, the parish council invited HRH the Princess Anne to come and perform the opening ceremony, with a bunfight in the Community Centre afterwards.

When I entered the hall, she was standing alone at the Top Table, as apparently no one had the confidence, or cheek, to approach her. So I went straight up to her and welcomed her to the village, just as though I were greeting a newcomer to the church, and a conversation ensued quite easily. She was, and still is, one of the Royals for whom I have a great deal of respect, particularly for her charitable work, sporting achievements and the way in which she bore herself during her personal problems. So we chatted quite amicably. She asked how many parishes I had the care of, and when I replied five, which was the case then, she replied she thought that was rather 'over-egging the custard'.

And so we continued talking, quite naturally over a cup of tea, of shoes and ships and sealing wax, and cabbages and kings, as Lewis Carroll might have said, until our conversation was drowned out by the arrival of her helicopter on the adjacent playing field, to whisk her away.

Lord Crawshaw's younger brother became High Sherriff of Leicestershire for one year, and asked me to be his personal chaplain. This ceremonial post mainly involved going with him to greet the arrival of the Crown Court Judge at the beginning of the sessions in Leicester Crown Court. So we would drive early in the morning into Leicester, and change into our ceremonial attire, and then go in police convoy to the Judge's Quarters, where he had stayed overnight. After collecting him, we were driven to the Cathedral, where we would process in for a service of welcome, which was mostly a variation on Matins, and I was expected to preach the sermon.

This was the most terrifying part for me – a country parson preaching in the mighty cathedral with cathedral staff, the Judge, the High Sherriff and officers of Leicestershire County Council present. I had to do this three times during my year of office, and was always at a loss to what I could say to such a distinguished congregation. A friend, and wag, with whom I was talking beforehand, suggested my text should be Matthew 7v.1 *'Judge not, that ye be not judged',* but that didn't seem quite appropriate somehow.

Then it was over to the court, where the Judge was welcomed with more speeches and ceremonial, and eventually we retired for a lavish lunch, at which the wine flowed freely. Then back to the court, where I was invited to sit on the bench with the Judge as he presided over the first of his cases on his list. Now after the excitement of getting up early, preaching in the cathedral and the rather lovely lunch, I was having trouble keeping awake by this time.

A nice juicy murder might have kept me alert, but it was inevitably a long fraud case, involving much legal argument, and while the barristers argued the niceties of the interpretations of the law to their heart's content, I sat in full view of everyone, struggling to keep my eyes open.

Our country churches were quite photographic, and one day I had a request from Brian True-May, a producer employed by the then Central TV, to use Diseworth Church for a funeral scene in the series 'Connie' which was based on the Nottingham Rag Trade, and intended for broadcast later. The PCC readily agreed, as it meant a sizeable contribution to their coffers, and the company sent industrial cleaners to subject the interior to a major clean up, involving scaffolding and heavy machinery – something far beyond the expertise of the loyal band of cleaners with their mops and buckets. They set up their tuck-wagon in the car park of the pub opposite, and seemed quite happy to feed not only the cast and production team but all and sundry during the three days they were filming, and many of the local residents soon learned they didn't have to bother buying food for half a week or so.

I naturally went along to keep an eye on things (just try keeping me away!), and was asked to sit at the head of the nave in my usual stall, to play the part of the officiating clergyman – a non-speaking part I must add! Filming was scheduled to take place over three days, and during one of the inevitable interruptions, I noticed one of the cast eyeing me, and she came up to me and asked,

'Are you a real one, or an actor?'

It was Stephanie Beecham, and during the ensuing conversation I asked her which had been her favourite of all the parts and programmes in which she had appeared. Without any hesitation, she replied 'Tenko – because I could just drop out of bed and go straight into filming, without the kerfuffle of getting dressed or made up'.

So the village church got a major clean and a handsome contribution to funds, the village got fed, and I got a lovely tale to relate to my grandchildren. And the three days' worth of filming, was edited into just a two minute scene, and when we tuned in our TVs a month or so later to watch it, we found that even that had not survived the final cut, as it was omitted altogether.

My fourth name to be dropped (and I promise this will be the last) also involves Diseworth Church. I was taking a couple I had been asked to marry through the ceremony the night before, with the couple, the bridesmaids, chief usher and all the usual suspects present, with the exception of the Best Man. The groom kept assuring me the Best Man knew exactly what to do and it would be fine on the day. He also had a curious glint in his eye, which I didn't think any more of at the time.

Come the day and the hour, and who should walk into the vestry to introduce himself, looking very much the part in kilt and full regalia, but Richard Wilson.

Somehow I managed to resist exclaiming 'I don't belieeeeve it!', and I think he was relieved I had, for we had an interesting conversation about his acting achievements to date and aspirations for the future. I was rather disappointed when the bride turned up almost on time, as Richard had to tend to his duties with the groom, and I had a marriage to conduct.

Postscript

A few years afterwards, Madeleine was taken into hospital with severe pain, and after much examination was diagnosed as suffering with ovarian cancer. There then followed a hectic four or five months, during which I drove her to various hospitals and clinics in the East Midlands for intensive courses of chemotherapy and radiotherapy, and every other therapy imaginable, before it was sadly concluded her cancer was too far advanced and it would be palliative care only from then on. Everyone was brilliant.

With the blessing of the Bishop I gave up most of my ministry to nurse and tend her at home. She bore everything very bravely, only going into a hospice for the last two weeks or so. When I said to her, 'You've never complained "Why me?"' she replied, 'And why not me?'

Six months after it was concluded there was nothing more they could do, she died, aged 46. We'd had six months to put our affairs in order and to say all we wanted to say and I suppose I must be grateful for that. Her death left me feeling totally numb and confused – feeling guilty there had been nothing else I could have done, devastated she was no longer with me, and yet relieved for her sake that it was all over.

Of one thing I was sure – I would never be as happy again.

Which just goes to show, and not for the first time in my life, how wrong I could be. For I met and married Judith, and have never regretted it.

But that, as they say, is another story.

In my sailor-suit, fastidiously checking the levels of the window bottoms of the premises on Sutcliffe Buildings, Wakefield Rd, Sowerby Bridge – not that the neighbours appreciated my hard work on their behalf

Acknowledgements

My particular thanks go especially to Lorna Gray at Crumps Barn Studio for her thorough editing of this script and for all the gallons of midnight oil she must have burned, and yet still remains remarkably sane at the end of it. And also to Judith, my present wife and artist, who gave much encouragement and acted as picture editor using her particular artistic skills, and was always ready to pour the necessary glass of merlot at the end of a difficult day.

This is obviously only a potted history of my life so far. I have deliberately avoided naming many people for fear of offending the many others whom I've inadvertently omitted. To them all, who gave me such happy and treasured memories and put up with me as their fumbling parish priest when their lives were hard enough already, I give my heartfelt thanks.

Printed in Great Britain
by Amazon